Armchair Traveller
at the bookHaus

JONATHAN CLEMENTS is the author of many books about China, including *The Art of War: A New Translation* and biographies of Chairman Mao, Marco Polo, Khubilai Khan and the Silk Road explorer Gustaf Mannerheim. His biographies of Empress Wu and the First Emperor of China have both been translated into Chinese. He was a consultant and interviewee on the National Geographic documentary *Koxinga: A Hero's Legacy*, which drew heavily on his book *Pirate King*, and has appeared on many other TV programmes on Asian history, including *New Secrets of the Terracotta Warriors* (broadcast in the US as *Emperor's Ghost Army*) and *Treasures of the Jade Empire*. In 2016, he was the presenter of *Route Awakening*, a TV series for National Geographic on the historical origins of Chinese cultural icons. His recent books include *Modern China: All That Matters*, an introduction to contemporary issues in the People's Republic, and *An Armchair Traveller's History of the Silk Road*, a guide for tourists in the Xinjiang region.

# An Armchair Traveller's History of Beijing

Jonathan Clements

Armchair Traveller
at the bookHaus

First published in Great Britain in 2016 by
The Armchair Traveller at the bookHaus
70 Cadogan Place, London SW1X 9AH
*www.thearmchairtraveller.com*

Some parts of this book previously appeared in *Beijing: Biography of a City*
(Sutton, 2008)

Map on p. vi created by Martin Stiff

A CIP catalogue record for this book is available from the British Library

ISBN: 978-1-909961-27-2
eISBN: 978-1-909961-30-2

Typeset in Garamond by MacGuru Ltd

Printed and bound in the Czech Republic by Akcentmedia

For Julie Makinen

# Beijing Subway Plan
# for 2016

Note: The two "Guanzhuang"s are of same pinyin, but different characters. The Guanzh of Line 15 is "关庄" (simplified) or "關莊" (traditional), while the Guanzhuang of Batong is "管庄" (simplified) or "管莊" (traditional).

# Contents

*Acknowledgements*                                          xv

Introduction                                                xvii
Dynasties                                                   xxii

1: The Land of Swallows: Prehistory to 221 BC                 1
The Discovery of Peking Man                                   1
The Waste of the Bitter Sea                                   4
The Place of Thistles                                         7
Intrigues of the Warring States                               8
The Plot to Kill a King                                      13

2: North and South: 221 BC–AD 1215                           16
Beijing as a Borderland                                      17
The Ballad of Mulan                                          19
The Life and Death of Nezha                                  22
South, Middle and Holy Capital                               23
The Bridge of Magpies                                        25

3: Khanbalikh: 1215–1368                                     29
The Chessboard Streets                                       31
The Tartar City                                              33
The 'Marco Polo Bridge'                                      35
The Drum and Bell Towers                                     36

4: The Forbidden City: 1368–1644                             39
Perpetual Happiness                                          39
The Living God of Wealth                                     41
The Centre of the World                                      44
The Eight Great Sights                                       50
The Advent of the Manchus                                    53

**5: 'Peking': 1644–1912**     55
A Square Atop a Rectangle     56
Lanes and Alleys     58
Foreign Mud     60
The Origin of 'Peking'     67
The Empress Dowager     68

**6: Northern Peace: 1912–1949**     74
The 100-Day Empire     75
The May 4th Movement     77
The People's Republic of China     80

**7: Empty Spaces: 1949–1989**     82
Permanent Revolution     83
The Underground City     86
The Goddess of Democracy     91

**8: Beijing in the 21st Century**     94
The 50th Anniversary     96
The Demolition Derby     97
Modern Ghosts     100
Interesting Times     102

**9: Eating and Drinking**     106
Food     106
Drink     109
Alcohol     110

**10: Travel Logistics**     113
Getting Around     114
Security Issues     115
Shopping     116
Postage and Packing     119

**11: Gazetteer**     120
The Centre: Tiananmen, the Forbidden City and environs     121
Xicheng (West Central)     126
Dongcheng (East Central)     128
Chaoyang (East Suburbs)     133
Fengtai (Southern Suburbs)     136

Haidian (West Suburbs)                          137
Shijingshan (Western Hills)                     139
Further Afield                                  140

*Chronology of Major Events*                    143

*Further Reading and References*                148

# Acknowledgements

Parts of this book previously appeared in a substantially different form as *Beijing: Biography of a City* (Sutton Publishing, 2008). Neither subject nor author is the same eight years later. The volume you are reading is considerably larger and draws on much new development in China's capital, particularly the growth of its subway from a mere two lines to today's fifteen-plus, and the new ease this affords the tourist for getting around. Professor Li Qi, of Xi'an Jiaotong University, made my visits much easier by appointing me a Visiting Professor from 2013–16. For Beijing itself, advice and hints were at hand from Alicia Noel, Chris and Randa Westland, Wang Xue'er, and Qiao Zhilin, who so sweetly trawled second-hand bookshops in search of a copy of the *Lao Beijing Lüxing Zhinan*. I also gratefully acknowledge the work of 'Hat600' for his efforts not only in compiling an up-to-date English-language subway map, but in making it available under a creative commons licence.

Julie Makinen and her sometime flatmate Lillian Chou were welcoming hosts in the diplomatic quarter, introducing me to the joys of Little Russia, the Central Business District and the hippest of hipster hutongs. Louisa Lim and Amy Li Xuebai invited me to their restaurants, Southern Barbarian (Yunnan food, now sadly gone) and Pak Pak (Thai food, hopefully still there), and discussed the intricacies of running a business in Beijing – skulduggery, bribes, double-crosses and all. On many occasions, I have been accompanied by friends, relatives and colleagues, whose whims and caprices have often dragged me to places I would not have otherwise been: Kati Clements, Andrew Deacon, Philipp and Sara Holtkamp, Raija and Matias Mäki-Kuutti, Timo and Seija Mäki-Kuutti, Henri Pirkkalainen and Tino Warinowski. My son Alexander has spent much of his young life in China, and was never a burden on our explorations of the city together, leading me into many new and unexpected encounters, including the time he was savaged by a rabbit at the zoo and the time he decided to rush the security fence at Mao's Mausoleum.

# Introduction

WANGFUJING, BEIJING'S BEST-KNOWN shopping street, is wide and pedestrianised, dotted with interactive sculptures of merchants, artisans and musicians. It is the only street in the world where a visitor can get his watch fixed (at the Hengdeli watchmakers), dine on Beijing duck and/or a scorpion kebab, shop for nappies in the Children's Store, and bungee-jump from the roof of the Lisheng sports store.

Despite its sanitised, modern convenience, and its thick population of shopping malls, Wangfujing is steeped in history. The street boasts two museums, unnoticed by the casual stroller – an archaeological exhibition of Palaeolithic hunters, hidden inside the Oriental Plaza, and the Beijing Arts and Crafts Museum, tucked away on the fourth floor of an unassuming shop.

Somewhere near the Apple Store, Stone Age hunters once tracked deer through a lost forest. Just over the road from the Donglaishun hotpot restaurant, a Manchu prince made his fortune by sinking one of the city's few reliable wells.

St Joseph's Catholic Cathedral is actually the fourth church on that site. Where skateboarders now mill and leap in its courtyard, 'Boxer' rebels once charged with firebrands and swords, intent on murdering the Christians who had sought sanctuary within.

Wangfujing has not always been known by this name. For a period of the 20th century, it was called Morrison Street, named for George Morrison, the Australian journalist who became an adviser to several Chinese presidents. Morrison's house once stood here, although its location was bulldozed long ago to make way for the Beijing Department Store. This, too, was once a site of historical importance, the first such shopping experience in the Communist capital.

There is a statue outside, but it is nobody you have heard of. Chairman Mao is not celebrated here, nor is Premier Zhou Enlai, who had his portrait taken at the studio across the street. There is not even a statue to George Morrison, despite all he did for China – the street lost his name in 1949.

Passers-by might assume that the bronze bust of the laughing man, broad-shouldered in a suit, is some sort of politician, or perhaps a vainglorious entrepreneur sticking his own effigy outside his main branch. But it is none of these things. The statue outside the Beijing Department Store is Zhang Binggui, the man who used to run the candy counter.

In 1950s Beijing, if there were sweets to be had, Zhang was the man who sold them. He always had a ready smile for his customers, and a savant-like skill to weigh a handful of candy without recourse to scales. This stood him in good stead when a big shipment arrived – on the shop's busiest-ever day, he sold two tonnes of candy in just three hours to a scrum of eager customers.

An understandable hit with the kids, Zhang Binggui was proclaimed to be a model worker of the People's Republic. He became the subject of children's books about hard work and good manners. His picture appeared in national periodicals. He died in 1987, and his son still runs the counter in his father's jovial style. You can go there today and buy half a kilo of gobstoppers.

There is something about the statue of Zhang Binggui that encapsulates the charm of Beijing for me. Cynics may scoff at the grandstanding and consumerism; doubters may smirk at the sop thrown to the little people, in a country that still boasts mountainous images of dictators and warlords. But there is something touching about the choice in priorities, and in the assertion, often repeated in Communist iconography, that the people are the heroes now. Zhang sold liquorice laces and humbugs for a living, and they built a statue to him because he made the children smile.

THE MING- AND QING-ERA historical city of Beijing is entirely contained within the 5km radius of the Second Ring Road, which follows the route of the old city walls. However, Beijing municipality covers 16,000 square kilometres and has an official population of 21.5

million – it is likely soon to out-people the whole of Australia. Its earliest archaeological relics of human habitation are half a million years old. In other words, it is no ordinary city, and any concise account such as this one faces an impossible task. I have chosen to focus on several key transformations in Beijing's history, in order to give the armchair traveller and real-world visitor a firm grounding in the way the city came to be. In the chapters that follow, you will read of the city's forgotten past as a kingdom in its own right, its centuries as little more than ruins, and its restoration as the capital of a Khan, the seat of Emperors, and the prize of warlords. Closing chapters deal with the city's recent past as the headquarters of Chinese Communism, and its meteoric modernisation in the last thirty years.

In keeping with the layout of other books in the Armchair Traveller series, there are also sections on the development of local cuisine, travel tips, and a gazetteer of notable tourist sites.

'ONE OF THE LURES OF PEKING', wrote the British traveller Mrs Alec Tweedie in 1926, 'is old temples, old gates, massive walls of ancient days, and another is the street life. That life is always new, varied and wonderful. Every day one sees something one has never seen before, and every day one enjoys it more. It is all so unique, so unlike anywhere or anything else. Its passing is sad. Poor, dear, dirty, tumble-down, peeling Peking.'

There are many guides to Beijing and all tell the same story. Chinese tradition rarely recognises an inherent value in a mere building – houses and palaces are often nothing but bricks, beams and tiles, liable to burn or fall down, and easily replaced. It is a location itself, its natural features and history, which endures. In their book *In Search of Old Peking* (1935), L.C. Arlington and William Lewisohn lamented the difficulties of writing an accurate guidebook to Beijing, and the possibility that readers might become irritated when they were unable to find monuments or buildings about which they had read:

> This, unfortunately, is not the fault of the authors – they would
> be only too glad if it was – but is due to the indifference of the
> Chinese themselves, more especially of their authorities, towards
> the historical monuments in which Peking is so rich. The loss by
> vandalism and utter neglect has been proceeding at such a rate

that, on repeated occasions, buildings and historical monuments
have actually disappeared while the authors are still writing
about them.

Their complaint is a common one, repeated throughout history.
Singers of the Dark Ages lamented the overgrown ruins of what
had been the capital of the Land of Swallows. Retreating Mongols
bemoaned the fate of their once-great Khan's City, doomed, or so
they thought, to fall into disrepair. In 2006, as I walked the dingy,
grey paths of a 1950s slum, my companion announced sorrowfully
that this, too, would soon pass, demolished to make way for Olympic
hotels. Perhaps, hundreds of thousands of years ago, Peking Man
looked over the rubble from his fallen cave roof, shook his head and
grunted that the place was falling apart.

When Arlington and Lewisohn wrote, they were scathing about
the removal of priceless treasures to the south. What would they have
said if they had known what we know now, that those same treasures
were not 'doomed to be eaten by moths, or destroyed by the damp'?
Instead, they were spirited away to Taiwan, where they remain,
regarded by some as an act of outrageous theft, and by others as an
act of fortuitous mercy. Had the retreating Republicans not taken the
treasures with them, they might have been destroyed forever during
the chaos of Mao's Cultural Revolution.

The early Communist era saw much of the old city demolished
to make way for modernisation. Palaces were turned into dormito-
ries; the city walls were pulled down to make space for a ring road.
Tiananmen Square, that internationally infamous void at China's
heart, is a relatively recent part of the city's mythos – the product of
town-planning one-upmanship during the Cold War, when Mao was
determined to have a parade ground to rival Moscow's Red Square.
The 21st century has seen even more invasive demolition, as entire
communities of old-fashioned housing are bulldozed to make way
for yet more shopping malls. As little as 4% of Beijing's traditional
buildings survive in 2016, and the bulk of those are concentrated in
the Forbidden City.

Over the last few years, I have experienced a frustration that
Arlington and Lewisohn would have found all too familiar. I have
written up notes on this street of artisans or that wonderful restaurant, only to return a year later and find them replaced by a Louis
Vuitton outlet and a kung-fu themed noodle franchise. But this is a

biography of a living, changing subject. This book will tell you Beijing's story – how the city has looked to thousands of generations of its inhabitants, its legends and its tales of rags to riches, to rags again and riches once more.

Despite its modern incarnation as the quintessence of China, Beijing sits at the crossroads of cultures. For many centuries of its history, it has not been a wholly 'Chinese' city at all, since some of its most influential denizens have been from cultures to which Chinese histories disparagingly refer to as 'barbarian'. It is only in the last century that we have seen a change in perspective that now regards all ethnicities in China as 'Chinese'. The likes of the Manchus or Mongols are no longer regarded as foreign philistines (as they are described in the annals of their enemies), but as subsets of a great melting-pot of 56 races, of which the 'Han' majority represent a 90% share.

Many such 'barbarians' were assimilated; some, like the Mongols and the Manchus, are indistinguishable to the average Westerner from the Chinese themselves. Such reversals of fortune have led to multiple name-changes over the years – Beijing has been the South Capital, Tranquil City, Northern Peace, the Middle City, the Great Metropolis, the Place of Thistles and the Bitter Sea. In an effort to keep things simple, I refer to it throughout this book as Beijing, 'North Capital', even though it did not really gain that distinction until 1403.

# Dynasties

MANY GUIDES TRANSLATED for foreign visitors still assume that the tourist knows their Ming from their Qing. It is hence worth acquainting oneself with the broad spread of the Chinese dynasties, not so much for understanding this book, as for appreciating some of the asides and short-hands of the average tour guide or museum signage.

These are the ones that are relevant for a visitor to Beijing:

## Ancient China

| | |
|---|---|
| Zhou Dynasty (time of Confucius) | 1100–221BC |
| Qin Dynasty (time of the First Emperor) | 221–207BC |
| Han Dynasty (China as a huge empire) | 206BC–AD220 |

## Early Medieval China

| | |
|---|---|
| Sui Dynasty (China reunited) | 581–618 |
| Tang Dynasty (height of the Silk Road) | 618–907 |
| Song (North and South) | 960–1279 |
| Liao (north including Beijing ruled by Khitans) | 916–1125 |
| Jin (north including Beijing ruled by Jurchens) | 1115–1234 |

## Late Medieval China

| | |
|---|---|
| Yuan (conquest by the Mongols; Beijing falls in 1215) | 1271–1368 |
| Ming (capital moves to Beijing in 1403) | 1368–1644 |

## The Modern Period

Qing (Manchu conquest, Empress Dowager, Last Emp.) 1644–1912
Republic (Yuan Shikai, Sun Yatsen, Japanese invasion)*    1912–1949
People's Republic (Chairman Mao et al.)        1949–present day

---

*The Republic of China continues on Taiwan to this day.

# The Land of Swallows: Prehistory to 221 BC

H E IS BARELY HUMAN. The nose is a little broader than one might be used to. The lips seem oddly thin, pressed in the beginnings of a smirk. Bushy eyebrows sit atop large brow ridges. He stares down the steps, towards what is now the car park, and seems lost in thought.

This is no ordinary sculpture. The bronze head that sits outside the Zhoukoudian museum is based on painstaking archaeological reconstruction. The artist Lucile Swan, a graduate of the Art Institute of Chicago, had moved to China in 1929, and found herself charged with the job of rebuilding the image of a man from mere fragments of bone. It was not the only sculpture that Swan worked on in Beijing. She also modelled a bust of Pierre Teilhard de Chardin, a Jesuit priest with whom she fell in love. They never consummated their relationship, although their passionate, heartfelt correspondence survives, as does Swan's statue of the famous 'Peking Man'. Today he stares, inscrutably, down the steps that lead up to the museum built in his honour.

## The Discovery of Peking Man

Only a hundred years ago, Zhoukoudian (see Gazetteer: Fengtai) was still an obscure mining community on the outskirts of Beijing, where residents quarried the nearby limestone hills. One cliff, known as Chicken Bone Hill, was notorious for its endless supply of old animal remains. Nor were its artefacts always readily recognised – it also contained many fossils of unidentified creatures, written off by local authorities as 'dragon bones'.

Still beyond the reach of the modern subway network, Zhouk-oudian doesn't attract the same dutifully trudging crowds as the Forbidden City. There are no truant students here trying to press-gang me into looking at their art show. No old ladies push postcards or souvenir fans. Zhoukoudian is a way out from the urban centre and chiefly of interest to archaeologists. On the day that I arrive, the car park is deserted. I have the gift shop to myself, the road to the summit is deserted, and at its terminus, I am the only man in the cave where the first men once dwelt.

A few foreign archaeologists picked over the area in the early 20th century and carted off some debris to analyse. It was not until 1926, in Sweden, that scientists picking over some Zhoukoudian junk made the discovery of a lifetime – two human teeth. The first documented case of *Homo erectus pekinensis*, or 'Peking Man' had already travelled thou-sands of miles from the place where he, his ancestors and his distant descendants had made their home for tens of thousands of years.

A wide, clean road leads up the hill to the museum, flanked by memorial tablets to the scholars who excavated Peking Man and his artefacts – men such as Johan Gunnar Andersson, the Swedish geologist who surveyed the hill in 1918, Pei Wenzhong, the Chinese archaeologist who found the first skull in 1929, and Pierre Teilhard de Chardin, the French palaeontologist who was denounced by the Catholic church as a heretic.

A path winds away from the low, unobtrusive museum around the hilltop itself, where cavemen spent thousands of years looking down on the valley below. A single glance is not enough to appreci-ate its full impact. It is not the cave that is impressive, but the fact that primitive man lived here for thousands of years. This bare cavern could be the very place where fire was first kindled; where the first words were spoken; where the first art was created in China. Like the Great Wall, it is not so much the sight itself that is humbling; it is the knowledge of how far it extends beyond view, out past the horizon, across the mountains and deep back into time.

Time, not mere hours and days, but *geological* time, has changed this environment. A once-great river, where Peking Man fished and paddled, has shifted hundreds of miles to the south. Many of the caves have been carefully torn apart in the interests of science, and are only now being restored to their previous state. But *which* previ-ous state? Here there was once a soaring, vaulted hall of shadows, the limestone walls sweating with spring water, a place used by generations of animals in search of a safe den. Millennia later, it was a split-level caveman apartment, its lower reaches used for burials and refuse.

Standing at the lowest point of the Zhoukoudian excavations, you gaze upward at a towering rock face, layers marked with occasional numbers. What was once a great cavernous fissure, as high as a football pitch is long, has slowly filled up over the centuries. At its lowest level, there is nothing save scattered lumps of ancient hyena faeces, scuffed and ground into the rock. But after thousands of years of occasional hyena habitation, the cave gains a new coating of red silt, as if new rains have washed mud from a new river somewhere nearby. Amidst the sandy clay are pieces of human fossil, animal bones and pieces of stone worked into scrapers and primitive axes.

Five hundred thousand years ago, Peking Man had arrived. The area was a lush, secluded valley, rich in game and plants. Peking Man hid from leopards, sabre-toothed tigers and bears, in an environment that was a home to porcupines, woolly rhinoceros and gazelles. He hunted these animals, luring the larger ones into a cave with a sudden vertical drop where he could finish them off at his leisure, cooking their meat on the first fires, scraping their skins to make the first rudimentary clothes. 'Suddenly', if anything can be sudden in geological time, Peking Man lost his furry covering and became a naked ape in need of animal skins to keep out the cold. He had become Upper Cave Man – *Homo sapiens*. Us.

Some have been harsh about Peking Man's culture. He has been accused of being a scavenger, not a hunter. His rudimentary, 'chopping' stone tools have been unfavourably compared with the 'axes' of his European cousins, although recent research has suggested that the easy availability of bamboo in China probably led to much more sophisticated tools that rotted away many centuries ago.

It has been suggested that he did not master fire quite as early as some believed. Of the human remains at Zhoukoudian, 40% are those of children under 14 years of age. Only 2.6% made it to fifty. His living arrangements have been ridiculed by modern observers who note not the fact of his survival, but the seemingly endless centuries in which so little changed, and early man huddled in the draughty, smoky gloom, chewing on the dirty, half-burnt, half-raw carcasses of bats.

One day, the sky fell in. The roof collapsed, leaving half the former cave open to the sky. The tribe of Peking Man relocated to the caves which still offered some protection from the outside world. He lived there for another eleven thousand years.

## The Waste of the Bitter Sea

There is something truly daunting about the history of Beijing – a place inhabited by mankind since before they were men, for literally hundreds of thousands of years. Ruins on the landscape mark the places where ancient reasons for habitation have disappeared – mighty rivers have changed their courses, and place-names recall the locations of dead springs, dried-up lakes and forgotten boundaries. There are hills in the Beijing area created by human hands; using soil and rocks dragged up to make great lakes. Beijing is also the place where sub-human savages fought with bears and hyenas for shelter in mountain caves, where some of the first men hid from beasts now extinct.

When the distant successors of Peking Man were able to talk, they told stories about their forebears. The Chinese sage Confucius, among others, recognised that the ancestors of the Chinese had lived like beasts, cowering in the dark from the winter cold, and sleeping in trees during the summer heat:

> Formerly the ancient kings had no houses. In winter they lived
> in caves which they had excavated, and in summer in nests,
> which they had framed. They knew not yet the transforming
> power of fire, but ate the fruits of plants and trees, and the flesh
> of birds and beasts, drinking their blood and swallowing [also]
> the hair and feathers. They knew not yet the use of flax and silk,
> but clothed themselves with feathers and skins. (*Book of Rites*
> VII:1:viii)

The traditional centre of Chinese civilisation was far to the south in Luoyang, far along the Yellow River valley. But the Beijing region retained an important role in early Chinese folklore. It was, after all, inhabited for a long time. Thirty thousand years before the present day, Beijing was the place where Ice Age glaciers reached their southernmost moraine. It was the edge of the known world, looking southward to the plains of agrarian civilisation and north into the mountains, steppes and forests of the wilderness. According to legend, it was where man first tried to tame the elements, particularly fire and water.

There is a precarious cast to life on China's central lands. The Yellow River's floodplain stretches for hundreds of miles, creating a volatile environment in which the river can all too easily change course. Some of the 'smaller' rivers in north China have at times been part of the main course of the Yellow River, while some canals were actually dredged along the beds of forgotten, dried-up streams. Nor is water management a catch-all solution – the vast quantities of silt that give the river its hue and name are easily dumped on its bed and banks, allowing it to swell over dams and break through levees, to the great danger of communities along its length. The result created a fear and respect for the mighty river throughout the time of Chinese legends.

The Beijing plain was almost uninhabitable for many centuries. Once the glacier snowmelt ran out, the rivers' continued retreat turned the lowlands into a brackish marsh stretching for many miles towards the sea, where reeds rocked in the wind across a long expanse of treacherous boggy ground. This, say the ancient legends, was the Waste of the Bitter Sea, home of a family of hateful dragons, who poisoned the surrounding area in an attempt to hold humans at bay. These dragons pop up on several occasions in Beijing's history, taking the blame for local natural disasters and reversals of fortune. Long into recorded history, Beijing's struggle for fresh water frequently elicited comments about the dragons in its midst, who must be opposed, appeased, avoided.

Chinese mythology is a garbled mass of stories about ancient conflicts between godlike beings and earthbound tribes. Amid the slow expansion of numerous animal-totem tribes, two warring factions eventually signed a truce. A man called the Yellow Sovereign, regarded by posterity as the ancestor of all the Chinese, led a confederation of totems, largely named after types of bear and big cat. They joined forces with another group, the Shennong people, possibly an alliance of nomad herders with pastoral farmers. This new confederation ran into another tribe somewhere in northeast China, where they fought over the precious resources of the plain of the Yellow River.

Accounts differ as to the identity of the rival leader. Some call him Shennong, using the name of the tribe with which the Yellow Sovereign's people had already merged. Others name him Chi You, and call him a son of Shennong. Whoever this individual was, he is said to have led over seventy different tribes into battle.

Ancient Chinese texts describe Chi You as a veritable demon, with horns on his head and fleshy bat-wings that allowed him to fly, leading an army of giants, Koreans and evil spirits. His 81 brothers supposedly had the power of human speech, but the bodies of beasts. To hear them described, they sound more like tanks, with bronze skulls, iron foreheads, and a diet of rocks and stones. He had the power to transform his appearance, and magical powers that permitted him to command the wind and rain in his service. Legend recounts that they met in a single colossal battle, although the events described go on for literally weeks and months.

The Yellow Sovereign charged onto a battlefield obscured by a magical mist, and was forced to fall back on sorceries of his own. He used a magnetic device to determine directions (said to be the world's first compass), and employed the services of his daughter, Drought Fury, to somehow desiccate the air. Even then, the battle was not over. Chi You himself was hunted down by the dragon Yinglong, who killed him, and was cursed to remain forever on Earth in punishment. The scattered remnants of Chi You's people fled far to the southwest, where, many generations later after many migrations, they evolved into the peripheral tribes known in Vietnam as the Hmong. To this day, Chi You is worshipped by the Hmong as a war god, and their term for him, pronounced in their own dialect as *Txiv Yawg*, means grandfather-ruler.

All this supposedly happened sometime around 2500 BC, on the plains close to where Beijing now stands. As the capital of the Yellow Sovereign, this legendary (and archaeologically unknown) Beijing was a symbol of the order that the Yellow Sovereign brought to Earth, walls against the elements and channels dug to carry water.

The story of the Yellow Sovereign is rich in water symbolism – spirits of rain, drought and flood warring for control of a world – the mighty torrents of the river rebelling against the farmers who thought they had tamed them. Not for nothing is the unpredictable Yellow River sometimes known as China's Sorrow, in memory of the millions killed by its sudden shifts in direction. But with the Yellow River turning southward, away from its former course, the region became less important.

But even if this legendary Beijing were a real place, it was soon marginalised in the eyes of the Chinese. The descendants of the legendary Yellow Sovereign moved ever westwards, eventually settling far upstream. Although the region where Beijing now stands was regarded as part of China by the earliest Chinese, it was still on the edge of the known world. As the legendary divinities of antiquity began their slow segue into a list of historical kings, north-east China became one of a handful of dukedoms that paid fealty to the rulers of the Zhou dynasty.

## The Place of Thistles

There is another forgotten conflict, unrecorded in the Chinese histories, but apparent from place-names. Where solid ground met marshland and lakes, facing the plains of reeds stretching towards the sea, there was a village called Ji, the Thistles. Its inhabitants were eventually absorbed into another group, the Yan – a picturesque name meaning The Swallows.

The Place of Thistles became a community within the Land of Swallows, named for the flocks of darting birds that can still be seen wheeling in its skies. Ji remained a town within the Yan domains, but a few hundred years later the conqueror's capital was abandoned in favour of Ji itself. Perhaps it was indefensible from northern barbarians, perhaps another well dried up, or floodwaters rose. Whatever the reason, Ji enjoyed a new lease of life – for the first time, the place we now call Beijing was the capital of a country.

These people of the Swallows made their home in and among the people of the Place of Thistles. Ji became Yan Jing, the Capital of the Swallows; a poetic name that can still be found sometimes on products and services in the Beijing area.

Its capital, identified from a handful of bronze artefacts unearthed to the south-west of modern Beijing, was a small enclosure, barely 850 metres across, encircled by an earth rampart. Archaeology has determined that the site itself was larger, perhaps two miles across, implying that the original fort soon attracted settlers who built their homes outside its walls.

The Land of Swallows was originally founded as a border-march – a place where a military garrison might watch the mountains for signs of invaders from the north. The Great Wall of China began life in the north of the Land of Swallows, although in a far less majestic incarnation than the one known today. Despite such potential dangers north of its borders, there were many periods in the history of the region where the supposed 'barbarians' were friendly, contained, absent or simply otherwise occupied. During such years, the state of

Yan was widely regarded as a paradise, insulated by its outlying location from much of the diplomatic pushing and shoving of other early
Chinese states. It was also blessed with good natural resources. Even
the mountains on its northern border could be refashioned as south-
facing agricultural slopes.

Su Qin, a famous diplomat from the nearby Land of Latecoming,
once observed that the Land of Swallows enjoyed such an abundance
of wild fruits and berries that its citizens could live for months on
end without troubling themselves over farming and harvests. Such
a comment, if anything more than a bit of political flattery, could
reflect the tail-end of the prehistoric cornucopia that may have first
attracted Peking Man to the region. Yan was the weakest of the seven
states of the era, but its alliance was highly prized for the security it
could offer for moving troops to other borders, contributing to war
efforts, and protecting the flanks of its neighbours.

It was widely believed, particularly among politicians, that China
was on the threshold of a new era. With the ancient lineage of the Zhou
kings now exercising little power beyond the walls of its own capital,
true power lay with their dukes. China was fated to enter another
cycle of civil war, and after an indeterminate period of fighting, a single
monarch would rise to subdue and unite the warring factions.

The Land of Swallows was spared much of the strife of the Warring
States – the main culprit behind the wars of the 4th century BC was
the distant Land of Qin, that dared not send an army against the
Land of Swallows for fear that other countries would use the opportunity to attack it from the rear. Over the years, however, the men
of Qin won battle after battle, and as the borders of the distant state
expanded, they grew ever closer to the Place of Thistles.

## Intrigues of the Warring States

Two countries were on a collision course. One was the aforementioned land of Qin, a harsh regime in the west, run on military lines
and geared for permanent war. The other was Qi, the Land of the
Devout, directly to the south of the Land of Swallows, determined
to become the overlord of the assembled kings – the word for such a
ruler, *ba*, weirdly endures today as part of the Chinese term for a Big
Mac (see Eating and Drinking).

During the fourth century BC, the dukes of China cast off their
loyalty to the powerless kings of the Zhou dynasty. Instead, each

proclaimed himself a king in his own right. Duke Yi (r.332–321) proclaimed that the Land of Swallows was no longer a vassal domain, but a fully independent monarchy. For the last two years of his reign, he was not a duke, but Beijing's first king, and his bold proclamation ushered in 101 years of monarchy.

Despite their claims of independence, most of the rulers of the former dukedoms entertained some hope that they would not merely prosper themselves, but dominate the others. They sought not to forget the Zhou kings of old, but to become just like them, absorbing their neighbours through means fair or foul, until one single autocrat dominated 'all under heaven' once more. The victor in that century of struggle would be the distant land of Qin to the west, the homeland of Duke Yi's wife. Cut off in its own remote valley, the state of Qin nurtured a project that was literally decades in the making, designed to create the perfect ruler, a ruthless conqueror devoid of any thought but domination, ruling an unstoppable state run on harsh and military discipline. The culmination of that bloodline would be born in 246 BC, and is remembered as the First Emperor of China. But in the hundred years that would pass before his victory over the Warring States, the other kingdoms jockeyed among themselves.

Even though it was stuck in its obscure corner, the Land of Swallows was soon embroiled in intrigues that characterised the period. With the death of its first king, his mourning period was not even officially over before the Land of Swallows was attacked by the neighbouring Land of the Devout, in a swift raid that seized ten cities on the countries' mutual borders. Su Qin was immediately dispatched as an envoy to the Land of the Devout, where he offered his congratulations to the king, and in the same breath, his condolences.

The king of the Land of the Devout was not expecting such a response, and pursued the ambassador across the throne room with a spear, demanding an explanation. Fearlessly, Su Qin told his enemy of what might happen. The Land of Swallows was indeed weak, but its marriage alliance with Qin gave it a friend in need – the leader of the most powerful and fearful army in the known world. The Land of Devout had snatched territory from its neighbour, engulfing it like a starving man grabs for food, but Su Qin warned his enemy that the territory he had just taken would be more like a deadly poison for the enemy who devoured it.

The story we have is from the *Intrigues of the Warring States*, a book emphasising the wily nature of diplomatic discourse. But Su

Qin's dialogue with the Land of the Devout is wholly believable. It was enough to make the Land of Devout return the territory, pay extensive damages, and offer a profound apology to both the Land of Swallows and its Qin allies.

Su Qin's younger brother Su Dai performed a similar role for King Kuai (r.320–314 BC). He, too, hoped to maintain the position of the Beijing region through intrigues, not military might. Su Dai was easily the match of his brother in such intrigues, and a consummate salesman, unafraid to put the tricks of pedlars and merchants to use in a courtly context. He was particularly fond of an old parable about a man trying to sell a fine horse, who stood, frustrated, in a marketplace for three days, without attracting any attention. For Su Dai, the quality of the horse might be of importance in a battle, or in a race, but it would not necessarily attract buyers in a market. The man in the parable eventually paid someone to shill for him, loudly 'noticing' the horse, praising its attributes, and lamenting that he wished he had the money to buy it, in order to attract actual customers. It was this sales trick that Su Dai was determined to put to use on potential rivals in the Land of the Devout.

When the Land of the Devout 'invited' minor Yan royals to visit, Su Dai advised his ruler to send them willingly – they might be hostages in all but name, but they would also be long-term guests, more liable to form friendships and political connections than to make enemies. Su Dai suggested that this would be even easier if Yan supplied the visitors with gold, silver and fine artefacts, so that they could bribe, impress and cajole their hosts.

The *Intrigues of the Warring States* record Su Dai's plans paying off in several diplomatic coups. Once, before arriving in the Land of the Devout for an important summit, he directly asked a Qi official if the man would play the part of the eager horse-buyer, planting stories and praises of Su Dai's greatness in the court, ready to make his arrival all the more impressive. Of course, Su Dai offered to pay his newfound friend's expenses, offering him a thousand measures of gold as 'horse's fodder'.

But ultimately Su Dai's prime loyalty was to himself, and his machinations would cause trouble for the Land of Swallows, particularly regarding his brother-in-law Zizhi, on behalf of whose promotion he was happy to play the part of the over-excited horse trader. Thanks to Su Dai and Zizhi, the Land of Swallows became a laughing stock among the Warring States, as the site of a supposed experiment in enlightened government, which ended in disaster.

The aging King Kuai lasted barely six years before he decided to abdicate his position – possibly through a combination of bad omens, bad luck and bad advice. Like many ministers during the Warring States era, Zizhi prized the message of an ancient folktale, in which the Yellow Sovereign's great-great-grandson decreed that the ideal person to take over his kingdom was not his biological heir, but his wisest minister. With the help of Su Dai, Zizhi persuaded the old King that the way to score the ultimate publicity coup against the Land of Devout, to shame them for all eternity and blind them with virtue, was to nominate Zizhi as his heir.

The other countries, it was argued, could not fail to be impressed with the Land of Swallows, whose ruler would become the first in recorded history to directly emulate the sage-kings of legend. Just as they had held off military might with words, surely such a decision would put them ahead in the race to be recognised as the rightful ruler of the world?

King Kuai had his doubts, but was assured that this, too, was another ruse. Zizhi pointed out that all the main ministers were supporters of the Crown Prince, and that of course, behind the scenes, the Crown Prince would still wield real power. The appointment of Zizhi as the new king would simply be an exercise in showmanship, for the greater good of the Land of Swallows.

It was a disaster. No sooner had King Kuai abdicated, Zizhi and his supporters did just as they pleased. Their power-grab lasted for barely three years before it was confronted with a mass uprising, not just by members of the general population, but also a large faction within the army, unsurprisingly in cahoots with the dispossessed Crown Prince.

While the rival factions were fighting each other, the wily Land of the Devout saw its chance, and sent its own army unopposed across the border. By the time the dust had settled, the usurpers were dead, but much of the Land of Swallows was under enemy occupation. After another year, the neighbouring Land of Latecoming, living up to its name, sent in its own forces, chasing out the invaders, and placing the hapless prince on the throne, as King Zhao (r.311–279 BC).

King Zhao had become the ruler of a land in ruins, and would never forgive the Land of the Devout for its opportunism. Nor was he particularly enamoured with the Land of Latecoming, a vassal state of distant Qin. An earlier ruler of the Land of Latecoming had assassinated a rival by smashing his skull in with a specially designed drinking goblet. It was, consequently, something of a racial stereotype that men of the Land of Latecoming were untrustworthy, two-faced brutes that were guaranteed to have ulterior motives. As King Zhao's new advisers saw it, his only hope of holding off an unwelcome return by his 'allies' from the Land of Latecoming was to go over their heads and contract an official alliance with his former enemy in Qin.

Another tale of the Warring States era credits Su Dai with the invention of a famous Asian folktale. He claimed to have seen a large mussel on the banks of the river that marked the border between the Land of Swallows and the Land of Latecoming. The mussel was attacked by a heron, and retaliated by slamming its shell shut, trapping the heron's beak. While the two animals remained locked in a stalemate, a passing farmer was able to catch them both. Su Dai likened the doubtful set-up of his fable to the constant warring of the minor states, and warned that Qin would be the sneaky farmer who stood to benefit from the strife.

King Zhao's long reign was characterised by a single project – his desire for revenge against the Land of the Devout. Ultimately, he would oversee the organising of a coalition which would pulverise the Land of the Devout in 284, invading on the flimsy pretext that the Land of the Devout had attacked an obscure statelet to its south. Unsurprisingly, its king had supposedly done so at the urging of a belligerent minister who had been bribed to suggest it by agents of the Land of Swallows!

The Land of the Swallows became a nominal partner in an international coalition, captured the enemy capital, and brought home the greatest prize imaginable. The Great Regulator bell was an item of great magical power, property of the kings of old, and said to confer universal kingship on whoever possessed it. Like several other mythical artefacts, the Land of the Devout had acquired it as part of the preparations for conquering all rival kingdoms. Now, it was taken back to the Land of Swallows, and sat in King Zhao's palace.

This gathering of the great and good, however, did not long outlast King Zhao himself, whose death in 279 was followed by purges and conspiracies that caused many of his greatest ministers and generals to flee to other countries. King Hui (r.278–272 BC) soon admitted his failings in a pleading letter to the exiles, begging for forgiveness, citing unfamiliarity with his new responsibilities, and a mistaken trust in his officials.

A better class of king might have served Yan better, but the last ruler of the dynasty did not learn from their mistakes. King Xi (254–222 BC) repeated the errors of his ancestors. To the west, the state of Qin's rolling conquest reached a terrifying height in the neighbouring Land of Latecoming, with a crushing defeat followed by a mass execution of literally hundreds of thousands of prisoners of war. Instead of regarding it as the portent that it undoubtedly was, all King Xi seems to have thought about was the opportunity this afforded him to invade his ruined neighbour.

King Xi was ready for war, but his general refused to consider an invasion even if his allotted troops were tripled in number. The angry king went ahead without him, and was forced to apologise after the well-trained, battle-hardened survivors of the earlier massacre were able to repel the invasion.

## The Plot to Kill a King

Despite dynastic marriages that had ensured the rulers of the Land of Swallows and the Land of Qin were cousins of some description, the agents of Qin were still bent on conquering the known world. As the counts of the borderlands had been elevated to dukedoms, and then claimed kingship for themselves, one king was determined to proclaim himself as the ruler of All Under Heaven. Regardless of family ties, the Land of Swallows risked being engulfed by the armies of Qin. Beset by famine in his own country, still suffering the shame of an embarrassing defeat in another quarrel abroad, King Xi was to be the last monarch of the Land of Swallows.

Tragically, King Xi had one of the best advisers of all. His own son and heir, the Red Prince, had actually been raised in Qin as one of the hostage-guests of the distant land. He had seen Qin's war machine at work first-hand, and had been a childhood friend of the man who had become Qin's ruler. King Xi, it seems, was content to replay the endless cycle of invasion and counter-attack, of insult and apology, which had characterised centuries of the Warring States. The king of Qin was playing an altogether different game, determined to proclaim himself as China's First Emperor.

More than two thousand years after the events described, it is difficult to assign blame. Possibly, King Xi was far more concerned about Qin than he cared to admit, but was placed in a position of plausible deniability by his own staff. But according to the historical record at least, King Xi had no part in the final solution of the Land of Swallows. Supposedly taking matters into his own hands, the Red Prince began a top-secret project to put a suicidal assassin into the king of Qin's throne room with a poisoned dagger. The assassin, a man called Jing Ke, lived for several years at the height of luxury and debauchery in the Land of Swallows, collecting, as it were, his payment in advance since he was unlikely to be alive to spend it afterwards.

Eventually, Jing Ke was dispatched to the land of Qin, travelling undercover as an ambassador. Behind him, the slave-girls, entertainers and servants who had attended to him for so many months were likely already dead, along with many of the Red Prince's trusted and devout agents, killed to prevent the secret coming out.

Jing Ke and his henchman were almost successful. After years of planning, months of travel, and days of waiting for the single perfect moment to strike, he got close enough to the king of Qin to snatch at his sleeve, diving for him with a dagger that he had kept hidden in a rolled-up map. But the king evaded his would-be killer, and the mission was a failure.

Jing Ke's mission has achieved a legendary status in the centuries since. His ill-fated murder attempt was the last thing that stood between the days of feudal China and the initiation of the imperial era, for the king he failed to kill would soon become the First Emperor. But there is something strange about the mission. If it were that secret, how do we know about it?

Jing Ke did not make it out of the king of Qin's throne room alive. He died slumped against a pillar, struck repeatedly by the king with a massive ceremonial sword. Possibly, the story of the plot was extracted by torture from his henchman, whose fate is not recorded in the history books. But otherwise, the allegation that the Red Prince initiated the project is merely circumstantial.

Whether or not it was truly a top-secret plot by the Red Prince, Jing Ke's brief scuffle with the king of Qin was to spell the end of the Land of Swallows. Using the assassination attempt as a pretext, the army of Qin launched an assault on the Land of Swallows, using the Land of Latecoming as a staging post. By 226 BC, the capital of Yan had been occupied by Qin troops, and the last king of the Land of Swallows had fled to the northeast. Although fighting continued for several more years, the state of Yan was no more. King Xi appeased Qin by handing over a suitable scapegoat – the Red Prince's head was sent to Qin, and soon after, King Xi himself surrendered.

The Land of Swallows was gone, along with all the other states. All under heaven was now unified in a single political entity, ruled by the First Emperor. China was born.

# 2

# North and South: 221 BC–AD 1215

THE PLACE ITSELF, and the meaning underlying it, is just over a thousand years old. The first building of its type in Beijing was built here in Ox Street in AD 996, although there is very little left of that first incarnation. It was destroyed by the Mongol invasion (see Chapter 3), entirely rebuilt in the Qing dynasty (see Chapter 4), and the area around it was thrice renovated in the twentieth century. The final change – for some, the final indignity – came in 2002, when the area around it was substantially 'improved', gentrified and de-cluttered to make a wider public space.

To the incautious observer, it might look like just another temple, but there are clues that this one is different. Compass in hand, you might notice that this does not face south like a Buddhist temple, but west towards a famous city far removed from China. There are, notably, no statues – the people who worship here place no truck in symbolic representations of human form. They have lived here for a thousand years – there are more than 20 million of them in China, forming such a prominent minority that they once had their own stripe on the Republican flag. The men are often darker-skinned than the average Beijinger and clad in little white hats; the women often veiled. Their shops sell mutton and *laghman* noodles, plum juice and middle-eastern candies.

Walk inside, and you are greeted by the black-bricked tombs of famous imans, and a cursive, alien script that proclaims: 'There is no god but Allah, and Muhammad is his Prophet.'

WHAT HAD ONCE BEEN the Land of Swallows became a mere administrative district. The earthen rampart to the north of the Place of Thistles was strengthened and lengthened, eventually linking up with similar ramparts in the Land of Latecoming, to form the first incarnation of China's Great Wall.

The Land of Swallows was never truly a kingdom again, although later centuries occasionally raised ghosts of the past. A generation later, within a few months of the fall of the First Emperor's son, a rebel in the region proclaimed that the Land of Swallows lived once more. He was killed by another usurper, and within a couple of years, the resurgent kingdom had been re-incorporated into the empire. The Land of Swallows reappeared again in AD 27, when the local prefect briefly enjoyed two years as a self-crowned ruler. For much of the early Christian era, the ruler of the region enjoyed the status of a king (*wang*), although the meaning of the title had been devalued in imperial China, becoming more equivalent to a 'prince'. Western China, closer to the new imperial capital at Luoyang, was ruled in a system of prefectures and provinces. Eastern China, including the Beijing area, was less tightly controlled, and often enjoyed a status more akin to tributary princedoms.

China's former kingdoms have never been forgotten. Throughout the imperial era, they lingered in poetic allusions and administrative divisions. Chinese astrologers divided the sky itself into nine areas, each believed to be a heavenly parallel with its earthbound equivalent – activity in the Yan quadrant, be it meteors or supernovae, was sure to be tallied with troubles in the area marked by the former borders of the Land of Swallows.

## Beijing as a Borderland

At some point, the region was inundated with seawater once more, turning hundreds of square miles into marshland. Just one of many changes in local features, the flood led to the rechristening of the area as *Kuhai*, the Bitter Sea, and to local stories that blamed the problem on those angry local dragons, unwilling to allow human settlers into their domain. The mischievous spirits were usually depicted as a family of four –the Dragon King and his wife, son and daughter – and town planning in Beijing remained dominated by concerns of ensuring an adequate water supply.

Despite this, the region prospered, attracting foreign immigrants such as the Xianbei, who settled in the Beijing area and refused to budge. Chinese historiography before the twentieth century had a habit of writing off all immigrants as 'barbarians' – conveniently forgetting the insult just as soon as the new arrivals have married into local families, adopted Chinese names, and settled down. Many parts of what is now called China were home to unique civilisations distinct from that of the 'Han' Chinese, but centuries of contact have diminished their local qualities. Today, there are but a few indicators of what were once very different cultures, such as the forked swords and alien statues of the native Sichuanese; the blunted, blocky pagodas that remain in the domain of the Xixia; the prominent Western noses of the descendants of Persian refugees in the hinterland; or the differing costumes and Muslim faith of the inner Asian Uyghurs. Similar cultural contacts appear to have been a feature of the Beijing region, where the local military developed a reputation for proficient cavalrymen, thanks largely to recruits from 'barbarian' immigrants like the Xianbei.

There are moments in the records where we can see the alien nature of Beijing life showing through. In the first century BC, three local men approached a magistrate from the south in a paternity dispute. The magistrate was aghast to discover that the three men all had the same wife, and scandalised when he realised that they had sought his aid because they had assumed he would regard their arrangement as completely normal. There were four children of this *ménage*, and the case turned on the question of who was whose. The magistrate observed that such questions of paternity and inheritance were precisely why Chinese tradition demanded a man should have a single wife, or at worst, a chief wife and many concubines. There was simply no provision in Chinese tradition for a single woman with many husbands, and such polyandry was regarded as a barbarian affront to Chinese decency. The shocked magistrate hence ordered the execution of the offending husbands, regarding their behaviour as 'inhuman'.

Whether the ruler was a prefect or a governor, a prince or a 'king', he was powerful enough to bring major changes. The Bitter Sea was brought back under control, with a network of canals dug for proper irrigation. Some of the worst of the marshes were drained in public projects that clearly benefited all. When an earthquake in AD 294 damaged the network, everybody pitched in on repairs – even the Xianbei regarded by the central government as unwelcome immigrants.

Perspectives, of course, differ. For many generations of Chinese emperors, the Beijing region remained a borderland, perilously close to the wild north, open to assault by any number of external tribes. But life looked different in Beijing itself, where the 'barbarians' were not a haunting, unknowable threat, but often relatives, trading partners, in-laws and friends. In what would become a feature of Beijing life for over a thousand years, the region enjoyed a dual status, not just as a north-eastern outpost of 'traditional' Chinese civilisation, but as a south-eastern centre for the outlying tribes. Not all were fierce nomads on horseback, although many were. To the layman, it would be extremely different to tell a Beijing barbarian from a Beijing Chinese – they ate the same food, wore the same clothes, and argued about the same things.

For a sense of this largely forgotten element of northeast Asian culture, you need only go to a Russian restaurant and ask for 'Siberian dumplings'. It is something of a shock when one's order arrives, and comprises objects indistinguishable from Chinese *jiaozi*, lacking only Chinese condiments. The dumpling travelled both east and west from Central Asia in the early Middle Ages, along with the durum wheat that was a vital component of both it and noodles – neither is native to China, and yet both are commonplace on Chinese menus, particularly in 'Peking' restaurants. Rice remained relatively unpopular in the north until at least the end of the first millennium – paddy fields used up far greater quantities of precious water than the administration could really afford, while the largely cavalry-based military complained that the boggy ground proved difficult for their squadrons to cross at speed. Even today, rice from China's northeast is a rarity – highly regarded and priced at a premium, not the least because the northern climate only permits a single crop per year.

For a brief period in the AD 300s, the ruler of the Land of Swallows was once more able to claim that he was indeed a true king, but this sign of the wavering of imperial authority carried implications of its own. The emperor's power was failing beneath incursions from new western barbarians, and when these attackers reached Yan, its renewed independence was crushed beneath a new imperium.

## The Ballad of Mulan

We see traces of this new culture in one of China's most famous poems, the *Ballad of Mulan*. Known today chiefly for its use as an inspiration for the Disney film, our modern image of Mulan is based on riotously anachronistic artistic licence. Style in the 1998 cartoon often leans on Han dynasty carvings, whereas the Beijing depicted in the film's finale owes much of its architecture to the Qing dynasty. But Mulan's tale probably dates from the 5th or 6th century of the Christian era, when north China was under barbarian control.

Presented at first like a poem of lost love, it shows a girl sighing at her loom, only to reveal, to the great surprise of many a tavern audience, that she is not pining from unrequited love, but from a desire to do her family proud by joining the army.

> Last night I saw the army notice
> The Khan calls up the soldiers
> Conscription lists in twelve scrolls
> And each one names a father.

Since Mulan is an only child, there is no brother to take her father's place in the conscription rolls, and she resolves to disguise herself as a man and join up herself. But the magic word here is *Khan*, not emperor. Although Mulan later meets him in person, and he is described later in more traditional terms as the 'Son of Heaven', the man with whom she is dealing is clearly not a traditional Chinese ruler. She serves ten years in a prolonged campaign, in locations as far afield as the Yellow River and the 'Mount of Swallows', before a grateful Khan offers her a government position.

> The Khan asks for her desire [but]
> Mulan has no need of high office
> 'Just a sturdy camel
> To take me to my distant home.'

The world in which the original Mulan serves is so alien to traditional China, so caught up in the Inner Asian worldview, that her mount of choice is a camel – this is usually forgotten in depictions of her, which if they show her with a steed, show her with a horse. And yet, she lives in a society advanced enough for her 'barbarian' town to possess four markets (a stylised description in verse five describes her shopping for her equipment), and organised enough to have roll-calls of conscripts. It is far removed from the Mulan of the Disney movie, who is shown *defending* China from such northern barbarians, who have climbed over the Great Wall and threaten the south.

Buddhism had also spread into China from India, and the new religion proved particularly popular among the northern tribes. In part, this may have been because they too saw themselves as new arrivals, but Buddhism also offered an escape route from the homespun, relentlessly parochial concerns of Chinese folk religion. This became particularly important in the early middle ages. China was reunited under the Sui emperors, who immediately flung their nascent realm's limited resources into a foreign war with the Koguryo kingdom of northern Korea – indeed, one modern retelling of the tale of Mulan suggests that she went on to fight in that war. In the Chinese fancy that life will imitate art, Beijing was renamed *Youzhou*, the Tranquil City, and functioned as the headquarters for a series of northward campaigns in the 6th and 7th centuries. The first campaigns were disastrous for China, and caused religious friction between Chinese popular religion and the Buddhism of the new aristocracy. Chinese folk beliefs held that the best possible life was lived at home, in harmony and tranquillity, and that a peaceful new existence awaited in the afterlife if one's corpse was safely returned to its hometown, buried with full honours, and appeased with regular ceremonial attention by one's ancestors.

This belief presented ample opportunity for religious dissent over the foreign wars of the new Sui emperors. Major defeats in Korea brought the Sui generals home, ready to fight another day, but they abandoned many thousands of their soldiers, left for dead on foreign fields, without proper burial, and with no hope of being transported home for the correct religious ceremony. The public backlash was a contributing factor to the swift demise of the Sui, overthrown by their cousins, the Tang dynasty, within a single generation.

Determined to avenge the Korean defeat, the Tang emperor Taizong arranged for Beijing to gain its first cenotaph in 645, the Temple of the Origin of the Law (*Fayuan-si*, see Gazetteer: Xicheng), where it was promised that monks would say prayers for the many war dead of the earlier campaigns. The founding of the temple was just one of several public relations exercises designed to bring the people around, but it failed to bring much luck to Taizong's armies. Fought to a standstill in Korea, he returned home a broken man. His successors were careful to appease both Buddhist and local beliefs, leading to several confusions. The most famous is probably the claim by the Empress Wu, who was a teenage concubine at the time of Taizong's death, that she was the earthly reincarnation of a Buddhist deity. But the clash of such different religious beliefs would also create new myths, one of which became part of Beijing's rich heritage.

## The Life and Death of Nezha

Buddhism brought with it a menagerie of new gods and demigods, picked up during the religion's spread through India, and co-opting many old Hindu deities into its pantheon. By the time Buddhism arrived in China, translation into and out of at least one foreign language, if not two, had wrought serious shifts in the interpretation of many scriptures. The snake- and elephant-inspired *naga* creatures of Hindu myth were transformed in translation into Chinese as *long*, or 'dragons', creating a tidal wave of new dragon stories to confuse local folk tales.

These 'dragon' legends became mingled with parts of a local story about a trickster god, to create a myth that became permanently interwoven with Beijing folklore. In the days before Chinese children were entertained by legends of the Monkey King, they heard about a child with super powers. After a long gestation period, Nezha was born to humble parents at an inauspicious hour of the morning. Cut from a fleshy sac by his irate father, the boy had three heads, each with a bonus central eye. He had eight hands, each wielding a golden weapon, and his whole body shone with an eerie red glow. Nezha could travel at great speed by riding on fiery wheels, and wielded a magic bracelet that could crush foes with the force of the entire horizon. Although some myths of Nezha appear to date back to the second millennium BC, many of the tales seem to have been fashioned in medieval times. Suggestions, for example, that he was the shield-bearer to the ruler of Heaven, the Jade Emperor, probably date from the 800s, when the Jade Emperor was officially adopted as the patron deity of the Tang dynasty's ruling house.

One of the most famous tales about Nezha records his conflict with a local dragon, which took exception to the churning of the river waters while Nezha was doing his laundry. A boundary dispute soon turned into an argument about who really ruled the area's all-important water, and ended with Nezha lifting his magic bracelet (usually depicted as something more like a metal hoop) and slaying the dragon with a single blow. The other dragons demanded restitution, leading to a feud between Nezha's exasperated family and the all-powerful creatures. Eventually, Nezha committed suicide to save his parents from having to pay any reparations, but his troubles continued in the afterlife. His mother built a temple to his memory, hoping thereby to ensure that he would be reincarnated – a Buddhist ending, tacked on a Chinese folk tale. His angry father, still intensely irked with his son's wild life and ignominious death, tore the temple down, leading a local priest to fashion a new Nezha out of lily stalks and lotus leaves. Eventually, the spirit of Nezha would be given a military post in Heaven, and there, the confused story should end.

However, over the centuries, the story of Nezha came to be associated specifically with the Beijing region, particularly in the later days of the Ming dynasty, when Nezha would offer supernatural aid to the city's architects. Although the location of the original stories seems sited in some vague dreamtime, the drift of the imperial family, Chinese religion and straightforward population numbers towards the north-east led many to assume that Nezha's story was bound to be associated with Beijing. But such assumptions would have to wait until the day that China was united once more.

## South, Middle and Holy Capital

For the four hundred years until 1368, Beijing was barely part of China at all. Its history went on, its trade continued, it stayed on the map, but its rulers were 'barbarians'. At the end of the Tang dynasty in 907, Khitan Tartars took control of north China, and Beijing with it. During this period, the ruins of the Great Wall defended the region from nobody. Nor was Beijing in the 'north' – in fact, in 938 it was renamed Nanjing ('South Capital') in recognition of its relation to other urban centres of the Liao dynasty – a ruling elite of Khitan tribesmen. The Khitans, wrote Putnam Weale,

> ...were a cheerful people, with a peculiar sense of humour and a still greater conviction of the inferiority of women. To show their contempt for them, it is still recorded that they used to slit the back of their wives and drink their blood to give them strength.

Chinese history books of this period usually claim that China was under the rule of the Song dynasty, but while 'real' Chinese history bumbled along in the south, and the emperors of the Song continued to call themselves the ruler of all under heaven, Beijing changed hands once more. Its new masters, in 1115, were a second Tartar tribe, the Jurchens, ('uncouth barbarians who soon drank themselves to death and destruction', observes Mr Weale) who ruled as the Jin ('Golden') dynasty until 1260, when they were ousted by still a third group of barbarians, the Mongols.

The names of the city continued to fluctuate. It was the south capital of the Liao, but was extensively enlarged and improved under the Jurchen, renamed the Holy Capital, 'Shengdu', and then the Middle Capital, 'Zhongdu' – a fair indication of the successful advance by the Jurchen armies, who marched as far south as the Yangtze.

China is a pragmatic civilisation. It works its magic on its oppressors, and it has time to do so. If Peking Man could exist for millennia in his caves, it takes but a blink of an eye for the Chinese system to ensorcel its conquerors. The initial days of any conquest were surely violent and dangerous, but within a few years, the temptations were there to appeal to a ruler's sense of snobbery and self-worth. Chinese princesses reared the next generation of half-Tartar heirs, and the new rulers inherited a bureaucracy dominated by Chinese. Even if the belligerent conquerors had wanted to lose themselves in administration, there would never be enough of them to go round. Despite their unquestioned military might and the unavoidable fact of their dominance, they still felt dwarfed by the cultural and historical heritage of the land they had conquered. It was not enough for them to rule this little piece of China, they wanted the whole thing, and it did not take long at all for them to hear of the Mandate of Heaven. If they wanted to gain Heaven's blessing for their planned conquest of the south, they would have to behave in a Chinese manner. Although the conquerors planned on clinging to their own religion, they were soon dragged into the seasonal cycle of the Chinese world, making sacrifices at the altars of Heaven and Earth, Sun and Moon. Tellingly, Beijing did not even possess such important sacred spaces – the Jurchen had to build them themselves, in imitation of those that they knew could be found far to the south in 'real' China.

Beijing's new masters had an inferiority complex about the 'true' Chinese capital to the south, ruled by the emperors of the Song. Accordingly, they enlisted the services of Zhang Hao, a Chinese architect, to turn the city of 'Zhongdu' into a Chinese-style capital that outdid the real thing. The Song capital of Kaifeng had grown organically over the centuries. It had developed suburbs beyond the walls, and strange kinks in its shape due to natural landmarks. Compare that to Beijing under the barbarians, almost a perfect square, oriented on a north-south axis in perfect keeping with the stipulations of ancient tradition.

The designs and sacred buildings of Jurchen Beijing were deliberately designed to recall the idealised chronicles of the forgotten capital of the kings of the Zhou Golden Age. By 1153, the 'barbarian' ruler of the Jurchen was worshipping in a Chinese style at altars built to ancient designs, and keeping Chinese-style ancestral tablets in order to pay homage to his forebears' spirits in special shrines.

He also adhered to Chinese superstitions. Although some temple pagodas might climb higher than a couple of stories, 99 feet was usually regarded as the maximum height allowable by the principles of *feng shui*. Good spirits, supposedly, flew through the air at a height of 100 feet, and any buildings in their airspace might impede their bestowal of fortune. As with so many explanations from Chinese geomancy, one is tempted to reverse cause and effect. It is, after all, far better to have the spirit world as an alibi, than it is to admit to a keen ruler that the tall buildings he wants in his own honour run the risk of collapse, earthquake damage and diminishing returns owing to their inhabitability in a pre-elevator age.

## The Bridge of Magpies

Beijing under non-Chinese occupation also saw the reassessment of certain old legends, such as that of Draught Ox, a straight line of three stars in what we would call the constellation of Vega, and the Weaver Maid, a triangle of stars in what we would call the constellation of Altair. Although the constellations were two of many in the ancient Chinese sky, the fact that an ox-drover was male, and a weaver female, and that the two stars were separated by the 'river' of the Milky Way, led later centuries to append a tale of star-crossed lovers who would be able to meet only once a year, on the seventh day of the seventh month, when a bridge of magpies would form across the river that divided them. The story of the Draught Ox and the Weaver Maid took many centuries to develop, but became particularly popular during the period of Jurchen rule over Beijing. On the seventh day of the seventh month, courtiers in Jurchen Beijing would wear badges showing the magpie bridge, supposedly in homage to the traditional festival, although possibly also out of a deep-seated sense of separation from the rest of China, south of the Jurchen border, eternally waiting for a fantastical remedy like the magpie bridge.

During the period of Khitan and Jurchen domination, Beijing's population seemed obsessed with other cities, particularly the life they imagined was going on far to the south, in a China that was not under foreign rule. Thoughts were on romantic idylls of an idealised, peaceful existence under the Song, or military schemes, eternally plotted and redrafted, for an eventual takeover. Chinese on both sides of the border speculated about reunification, and as the barbarian ruling class was diluted with increasing amounts of Chinese blood with every generation, the separation of these two Chinas seemed increasingly ludicrous. By the 13th century, the standoff between the Northern Jin and Southern Song was no longer a matter of a slow invasion, whose frontline had remained static for more than a century. Instead, it had become a contest between two rival dynasties for the favour of Heaven. North and South both strove to outdo each other in the ostentation of their religious services, and with their capitals' claims to be the Centre of the World. Such boasts were not made to each other in diplomatic communications, but directly to Heaven, in a constant struggle for a sign, some portent or astrological manifestation, that China would soon be unified once more. As part of this one-upmanship, the denizens of Beijing clung to their own ancient history, particularly Beijing's brief period as a monarchy, and the dimly remembered legends of ancient prominence. Even when the capital of China was far to the south, the people of the Beijing region still assured each other that the land where they lived and died had been the site of ancient clashes between gods and demons, and (ironically with some element of truth) where men had first walked the earth.

A folk tale of the period maintains a sense of yearning for a lost unity with the south, subtly buried beneath a traditional love story. The association of the area with the swallow continued, particularly with reference to the Terrace Where Swallows Muster, an earth mound in the countryside outside modern Beijing, where thousands of birds congregated each autumn. Flocks of swallows sufficient to darken the sky stay in the area for a few days, before beginning their winter migration south, to Hainan and points beyond. The sight of the birds, however, eventually generated a legend of its own, redolent of tragic medieval romances, Grimm's fairy tales and even a touch of Oscar Wilde, in the story of a rich landlord's daughter.

So the story goes, Hongbao ('Ruby') was persecuted for her inno-cent friendship with the son of a poor man. Despite her protestations that Xiao Yan ('Little Swallow') was just a friend, the girl was ordered never to see him. Her carefree childhood play was curtailed as she reached marriageable age, and she was no longer permitted to go outside. Imprisoned indoors with nothing to do but embroider, she amused herself by occasionally ditching the flower patterns she had been provided in favour of small and exquisite thread birds, which she would drop out of the window as gifts for Xiao Yan.

Her father hears her whispering 'Fly, swallow! Fly away!' and immediately assumes the worse. So might we, but centuries of fairy-tale retellings have reversed the likely truth of the tale – instead, we are told that one of her embroidered birds had come to life, and it was that which she was addressing. Her scandalised father, however, will not be persuaded, and instead bribes a local magistrate to exile Xiao Yan far to the south on trumped-up charges.

As Ruby pines away for her lost beau, she is visited by a lone bird, returning from the distant tropical island, and tweeting the worst news that she can imagine: that Xiao Yan has died in exile. Ruby asks the bird to confirm by flying three times around her house, which it then does. Ruby then cries herself to sleep, weeping tears of blood – standard Chinese hyperbole for misery, but here taken literally. When she inevitably dies of a broken heart, she is buried up on the earthen slope near her house – a place that soon grows with strange 'Swallow Grass', whose blood-red sap can be squeezed out and used to make dyes and cosmetic rouge. Thereafter, each year, the swallows return to the terrace and wait for two days in the vicinity of the grave, in case the spirit of Ruby has a message for them to take south to Hainan.

North and South would eventually be reunited, but not through any Chinese or supernatural agency. In the 13th century, the North was conquered by a new tribe of outsiders – the Mongols. Beijing put up a brave resistance to the approach of Genghis Khan – brave because the Mongols famously offered no quarter to any who refused to surrender. By not immediately opening its gates to the Mongols, Beijing's fate was sealed, and the city succumbed to a relentless storm of fire-arrows in 1215. The Mongols, their forces swelled by defecting Chinese soldiers who had originally been tasked with defending the city, crashed through the gates and put every living thing in the city to the sword. The surviving palaces were looted and set on fire, and by the time the army had passed, Beijing had been totally destroyed.

A surviving report of the immediate aftermath paints a terrifying picture. The fires reduced the buildings of Beijing to charred ruins, while men, women and children had died in such huge numbers that the streets were slick with human fat. Beijing was left to the buzzards, and remained a ghost town for several decades, until Khubilai, the grandson of Genghis Khan, completed the conquest of China, uniting the country for the first time in centuries, and proclaimed himself the first emperor of a new dynasty, which he gave the majestic and provocative title of *Yuan*: Beginning.

This new start solved the enduring problem of the rival capitals in North and South. The new ruler chose the location of the true capital. He chose Beijing.

# 3

# Khanbalikh: 1215–1368

A SHORT STROLL WEST from Mudanyuan station (Line 10), by the side of the canal that once formed the moat of his city wall, there is an imposing statue of Khubilai Khan. He sits on a throne borne by four elephants, flanked by two lissome women in the crooked witches' hats favoured by his mother and wife, and accompanied by a lithe, alert leopard.

Khubilai himself is incredibly fat. His bulk is so huge that he leans on his left hand, buttressing his upper body as if keeping himself upright is a chore even when seated. This is the gout-ridden, morbidly obese tyrant of the historical record at the moment of his greatest triumph: the foundation of the city of Khanbalikh in 1271. Stretching away to either side of him is an intercultural parade of minions – his Arab astronomer, his Nepalese architect, a Buddhist monk and sundry other foreigners, to hammer home the message of the commemorative plaque in front, that the Khan's great city was founded through the efforts of 'the people of all nations'. There is even a crucifix – a rare sight in China – sitting alone to one side in seeming recognition of his dabbling with foreign religions. It was after all, Khubilai who asked the Polo brothers to bring back great Christian minds to dispute with other religions at his court, so he could best decide which path to follow. Famously, they failed to turn up with any actual monks, but did lend him young Marco Polo as a servant.

Polo joined the 'persons of various categories' in Khubilai's service, alongside Uyghurs, Mongols and Jurchens, as well as the Chinese. One such local collaborator, Guo Shoujing (1231–1316), is largely unknown to foreigners, although his place in the history of Chinese science is unassailable. He is such a big deal that Beijing manages to have *two* statues of him – curious when one considers the propensity of governments to honour the rulers and despots, rather than the boffins who scurry to carry out their commands. But then again, Guo Shoujing was Chinese, and Khubilai Khan was a Mongol invader.

A child prodigy in the latter days of the Song dynasty, Guo found his true niche in the wake of the Mongol conquest, when Khubilai Khan put him in charge of repairing Beijing's infrastructure. He oversaw the repair of the Grand Canal, and the construction of an aqueduct to convey much needed fresh water to the capital. In his fifties, collating the data from dozens of observatories all around China, he reported on the true length of the year to the emperor. In his sixties, he was appointed as the head of governmental Water Works, bringing him into intimate contact with trade conduits and water supply issues. He was the most prominent scientist of Yuan-dynasty Beijing.

A broad head-and-shoulders bust of Guo can be found at his Memorial Pavilion at the far northern end of the Houhai lake, where his Baifu Canal once brought water 30km from the Baifu spring, through Kunming Lake at what is now the Summer Palace, and into the centre of Khubilai's capital. He wears a scholar's cap and has protruding ears, and lips pursed through his goatee beard as if he is just about to voice his disapproval. If he seems a little angry, it might have something to do with the constant carping directed at his achievements – it is frequently suggested that much of his work in mathematics and astronomy had been ripped off from Muslim scholars at Khubilai's court, although nobody has ever managed to prove this.

A second, more modest bust of him can be found in the grounds of the Ancient Observatory, close to where his Tonghui Canal left the city to connect to the Grand Canal 17km away. The beard is longer, but the scowl is still present.

In linking Beijing to the Grand Canal, Guo Shoujing transformed the city, integrating the capital into the Chinese system, but also making it possible for there to be a capital at all. At the time of his birth, Beijing still lay largely in ruins. The Grand Canal was vital in making it possible not only for a city to function, but for the workmen and materials to reach the city in order to rebuild it in the first place.

## The Chessboard Streets

When Khubilai Khan's architects began constructing what would be known as Khanbalikh, 'the Khan's city', they ignored the blackened, haunted shell of the old town, and built a completely new one on its northeast corner. Marco Polo wrote that Khubilai's astrologers had predicted the old town would rebel, and so encouraged him to weasel out of the curse by building *nearby* instead of *rebuilding* the site itself.

But while such folktales may have made for amusing fireside anecdotes in local taverns, they ignored more prosaic reasons for the move. The ruined city could have easily been restored, but the Mongols were planning for a much bigger metropolis. Beijing had been the meeting place of north and south for many centuries, but now Khubilai was to proclaim himself as a Chinese emperor, the first of the new Yuan dynasty, he would need more than just a regional capital. He needed a national nexus, and with such a plan came the expectation of a much larger urban population. Khubilai's city soon grew into one of the largest in the world, laid out with wide regular avenues that impressed all foreign visitors. The most famous contemporary account of the city is by Marco Polo, who wrote of the city of 'Cambaluc' in his *Travels*.

> All the plots of ground on which the houses of the city are built
> are four-square and laid out with straight lines; all the courts and
> gardens of proportionate size... Each square plot is encompassed
> by handsome streets for traffic, and thus the whole city is
> arranged in squares just like a chess board... In the middle of the
> city there is a great [bell] which is struck at night. And after it
> had struck three times, no one must go out of the city.

Polo was able to get a bird's eye view of the city by climbing the steps to the roof of one of the city's eleven gates (he counted twelve, but close enough). The city was smaller in those days, and smog-free, and Polo was able to see clear across to the opposite wall – the avenues were straight all the way.

The dragons of the Bitter Sea, those recurring characters of Beijing legend, would also have their say. The water supply for the old city was simply too paltry to support Khubilai's plans. It was far better for the Mongols to site their new capital on the north-eastern edge of the old town, where two rivers flowed into an elongated pair of lakes, the site of a previous royal park, before continuing on their way out of town. Khubilai's personal palace was built on the eastern shore of one of these lakes, which was dredged and expanded – the soil and rocks from the process dumped to the north to form the basis of what is now Coal Hill to the north of the Forbidden City.

One of the few remnants of the Mongol era survives in what is now Beihai Park where the serene and most northerly lake curves gracefully around Hortensia Island, once the private preserve of the Mongol emperors. Marco Polo described the park in its Yuan dynasty heyday as a paradise:

> Between the two walls of the enclosure are fine parks and
> beautiful trees bearing a variety of fruits. There are beasts also
> of sundry kinds, such as white stags and fallow deer, gazelles
> and roebucks, and fine squirrels... There extends a fine Lake,
> containing fish of different kind which the Emperor has caused
> to be put there, so that whenever he desires any he can have them
> at his pleasures. A river enters this lake and issues from it, but
> there is a grating of iron or brass put up so that the fish cannot
> escape in that way.

Polo may never have seen the park for himself, or if he did, only on a brief escorted visit. He does, however, have plenty to say about other pleasures on offer elsewhere in the city, and claims that Yuan-era Beijing boasted some 20,000 prostitutes.

Place names and folklore retain vestiges of many a drunken night in Beihai Park. Several *trees* in the park were awarded ministerial rank in old imperial governments, doubtless conferred upon them by sozzled rulers. Although a bridge now connects Hortensia Island to the rest of the park, in Khubilai's time it was only reachable by boat. A day in the park would end with boating on the lake in the sunset, and at dusk all the barges would be moored at the island, and the khan and his followers could spend the night with their women in a number of exquisite pavilions. For any consort who had managed to run a gauntlet of obstructive eunuchs and imperial caprices, a night trapped on Hortensia Island was a coveted opportunity; for any Yuan-dynasty beauty that did not want the attentions of an amorous emperor, it was a nightlong test of endurance.

The park was not always as tranquil as it seems today. Beijing folk-lore retains a story that may be the vestiges of a forgotten murder, or simply a groundless bogeyman to scare children. But, so the stories go, sometimes a black-cloaked man can be found in Beihai Park, offering to take late-night loiterers home. Instead of being a friendly old-world taxi driver with a donkey cart, the man is actually a ghost, determined to drag unsuspecting passengers down into his lair beneath the bridge, where he drowns them in the waters of the lake and feeds on their souls.

Resident in Beijing sometime in the 1280s, Marco Polo was a *semuren* – a 'miscellaneous alien' – one of many hundreds of foreign administrators employed by the Mongols to aid in running their newly conquered country. Most of the *semuren* were from Central Asia, and their number included many Nestorian Christians and Muslims, leading to certain anxieties at the capital. Matters were particularly tense over the subject of religion – missionaries from all major faiths, as well as a number of cultists and outright charlatans, were honoured guests at Khubilai's court, and kept permanently guessing as to the emperor's disposition towards them. All lived in hope that the Mongol conqueror would recognise their belief as the one ultimate truth, and drag the people of China along with him in his conversion. But Khubilai hedged his bets throughout his reign, refusing to come out for or against any one religion. His chief wife was a Nestorian Christian, most of his advisers Buddhists or Muslims, but Khubilai himself was careful to appeal to everyone.

## The Tartar City

The Mongols dwelt in the newly built area or 'Tartar City', while the old ruins and the formerly unoccupied land soon filled up with their subjects – the ruins were not abandoned for long, but soon attracted entrepreneurs and merchants who wiped out most traces of the old city. Few Mongols and fewer of the foreign *semuren* administrators were fluent in Chinese, and most communications among Marco's colleagues was conducted in Persian. It seems that Marco himself never learned more than a few words of Chinese, leading to many supposed 'errors' in his account of his travels. In fact, his experience of China was akin to that of a foreign diplomat on a brief fact-finding mission, forced to regard everything through the limited opportunities afforded for actual local contacts.

The centuries of north-south divide in China had created palpable differences, enough for Marco Polo to believe that China was two countries – 'Khitai', where Beijing was located, and 'Manzi' to the south. Ironically, the latter term was actually Chinese for 'south-ern barbarian', co-opted by the occupied north as a derogatory term for China proper. There are tantalising hints in Polo's account that someone sat him down on at least one occasion and attempted to explain how Beijing had been subject to non-Chinese rule for some time before the arrival of the Mongols. However, the story was easily garbled – determined to make themselves sound legitimate, the Jurchens had given their dynasty a Chinese name: Jin. As it literally means 'Golden', Polo seems to have confused this period (1115–1234) with an unrelated Jin kingdom two thousand years previously, and the close pronunciation of Qin, the dynasty of the First Emperor. This caused him to relate fanciful and muddled tales of a legendary 'Golden King' in the region, that were linked, probably by his own wishful thinking, to other stories of the fabled Christian king of Asia, Prester John.

Polo's description of the Khan's realm includes discussions of Muslim peoples, primitive tribes in the jungles, Indians, Tibetans and Turks. On rare occasions when Polo did deal directly with the Chinese themselves, he often found them infuriating – particularly the women, who were demure, graceful and entirely unavailable.

The most important development for Beijing during Marco Polo's time was the renovation of its Grand Canal. At first, the Mongols expected that grain fleets sailing up the coast of China, into the Gulf of Bohai and then upriver near what is now Tianjin could feed Beijing's hungry mouths. Pirates aside, the greatest danger was the weather, culminating in a disastrous sequence of events in the famine year of 1286 when a quarter of the city's grain was lost at sea in storms.

Partly out of a deep-seated mistrust of the open sea, and partly from a pragmatic desire to avoid pirates and charge enforceable tolls, the Mongols ordered the construction of a canal that would connect Beijing to the south. Khubilai made the renovation (in fact, recreation) of the old Sui dynasty canal his top priority, and sym-bolically reunited North and South with a critical waterway for the first time in centuries. Chinese rulers had dredged river transpor-tation corridors across the land before, but the Yuan dynasty saw a vast improvement. At the time of Marco's residence, the canal still stopped a way short of the metropolis itself, obliging merchants to offload their cargoes and wheel them the final few miles into Beijing on carts. Around 1293, shortly after Polo left China for his European homeland, the canal network was extended right to Beijing itself. It went up all the way to the east wall of the emperor's palace, and then around to the north, where it ended in a huge inland harbour, with ample docking facilities in the middle of the city. Some vestige of this Beijing 'port' survives today as the cluster of lakes at Houhai, now a picturesque district of bars and restaurants to the north of Beihai Park (see Gazetteer: Xicheng).

The Canal made it possible for grain barges to come all the way from the fertile south: from river system, to lake, to canal, to river system, without once having to head for open water. It was now feasible to have a capital in the north that continued to grow – the Mongols had planned sufficiently ahead, and their new, larger water supply and better provisioning ensured that Beijing grew swiftly.

## The 'Marco Polo Bridge'

Transport networks were improved elsewhere, too. To the west of Beijing, Marco Polo described a bustling market, where a sturdy bridge complete with churning water mills became the site of a trading post – with merchants unloading their goods ready for transhipment, but often hoping to save on cargo by selling them off right away.

> When you leave the City… and have ridden ten miles, you come
> to a very large river which is called Pulisangkin and flows into
> the ocean, so that merchants with their merchandise ascend to it
> from the sea. Over this river there is a very fine stone bridge, so
> fine indeed that it has few equals.

The river was known as the Sanggan from the 8th century onwards, but this appears to be a coincidence. His *Pulisangkin* is not Chinese at all, but simply Persian for 'stone bridge'. The Chinese themselves called it the bridge of *Lugou* ('the Cottage/Black/Lu Family Waterway'), but today it is known outside China as the 'Marco Polo Bridge' (see Gazetteer: Fengtai).

> The fashion is this: It is 300 paces in length and it must have a
> good eight paces in width, for ten mounted men can ride across
> it abreast. It has 24 arches and many water mills, and is all of a
> very fine marble, well built and firmly founded. Along the top
> of the bridge there is on either side a parapet of marble slabs

and columns made in this way: At the beginning of the bridge there is a marble column, and under it a marble lion so that the column stands upon the lions loins while on top of the column there is a second lion both being of great size and beautiful sculpture. At the distance of a pace from this column, there is another precisely the same, also with its two lions and the space between them is closed with slabs of grey marble to prevent people from falling over into the water. And thus the columns run from space to space along either side of the bridge, so that altogether it is a beautiful object.

In the 21st century, the Marco Polo Bridge has been carefully reno-vated. Some original paving slabs are retained in its central walkway, but for show only, so that modern visitors can gaze in awe at the wear and tear done to hard stone by centuries of footfalls from litter-bear-ers, porters and cutpurses. Stone friezes and statues at either end tell tales about the bridge's history, but they are clearly modern additions. So, too, are many of the stone lions that first attracted Marco's atten-tion. One only needs to look at the heads of the giant stone turtles, worn almost featureless by generations of attention from excited chil-dren, to see how a true Yuan-dynasty artefact is likely to look today.

## The Drum and Bell Towers

The period of Mongol rule saw the construction of drum and bell towers to match the city's expanded size. The absence of any form of readily available time-piece meant that the standard method of time keeping across the city, for merchants, priests and members of the public was defined by the sounding of the central towers. The drums were beaten in the morning to signify dawn; the bells rung at night to announce the formal end of the day – Beijing did not have a curfew as such, but anyone going out after the sounding of the Bell Tower would need a lantern to light their way, and a bodyguard to watch over them.

The Mongol Bell Tower was built in 1272, and stood for nearly five hundred years before its destruction by fire and replacement with the one that stands today (see Gazetteer: Dongcheng). But it is the Mongol tower that became part of Beijing's local folklore, its huge bell producing a surprisingly mournful, soft chime each evening, sounding to Chinese ears like someone whispering *xie, xie*.

Beijing children were told that it was time to go to bed, because the Bell Goddess was calling for her shoe (*xie*), a story that grew with the telling to become a tragic fairy tale of the bell's construction. An unnamed emperor (presumably Khubilai) ordered his Minister of Works to cast a ten-tonne bell, but was displeased with the iron monstrosity that was first produced. He told his craftsmen to come up with a bronze replacement in just three months, big enough and loud enough for its sound to carry as far as Beijing's suburbs.

Working under pain of death, the craftsmen faced great difficulty with their enforced materials. It was possible for them to cast bronze at such a great size, but they were unable to guarantee the finished bell would ring true. As attempt after attempt met with dull, unsuitable chimes, the workmen began to lose heart. On the day before the deadline, the lead craftsman's daughter arrived at the foundry, clad in her best clothes, and asked how the work was coming along. On hearing that the situation was still desperate, she flung herself into the molten bronze. Her anguished father was left clutching nothing but a single slipper, as his daughter sank forever into the agonising hot metal. Her death, however, supposedly brought about a great change in the quality of the bronze, leading to a miraculously clear tone on the huge bell.

Despite such desperate measures undertaken to create the perfect capital, Khubilai did not find Beijing wholly to his liking. He spent the hot summer months away from his new capital, far to the north at his secondary residence in Shangdu, the 'Xanadu' of poetic legend. As for the Yuan dynasty itself, it flourished only briefly. The conquering Mongol vigour was soon vanquished by the temptations of China itself – even as Khubilai proclaimed himself emperor, he was adhering to his own upbringing, which had deliberately favoured a Chinese attitude.

The Yuan dynasty did not last quite as long as the ancient Land of Swallows – Khubilai and his descendants were masters of Beijing for just under a century, from 1271 to 1368. Along with their conquests they inherited the same problems as their predecessors – the usual cycles of famine and plenty, health and plague. The Mongols changed China forever and reunited it after centuries of the North-South divide, but by the mid-1300s, China was suffering from droughts and plagues that made it seem as if Heaven favoured a new change in the ruler. An unidentified disease decimated the Chinese population in the 1330s, likely to have been the very same Black Death that would follow Mongol armies into distant Europe. The disease or something similar returned in an outbreak that killed millions between 1353 and 1354, exacerbating tensions among the survivors.

From the time of the first outbreak, the Mongol hold on China was slipping. Loyalties wore thin among the Chinese population that still greatly outnumbered their Mongol masters, and combined with superstition about the 'bad omens'. The simple struggle for survival did the rest of the job, leading to outbreaks of rebellion in the early-to mid- 1300s. One of the rebel groups eventually grew to present an effective opposition to the Mongols, and successfully chased the Yuan dynasty rulers out of their 'Khan's City'. As far at the Mongols were concerned, the Yuan dynasty continued for many more centuries, but the extent of its territory did not include China.

China, the 'Khan's City' included, now fell under the leadership of a new 'dynasty of Brightness' – the *Ming*. For a brief moment, it seemed as if Beijing would lose its old status, reverting to a peripheral town as the power base in China shifted back south. Instead, Beijing's position was strengthened and reaffirmed, almost by chance, and the city was rebuilt once more – improved beyond all recognition.

It was in the Ming dynasty that Beijing's all-important central citadel truly took its modern shape. Building on the start made by the Mongols, the new rulers of Beijing would refine their capital to create one of the most stupendous sights in the world – an entire city within a city, designed for the imperial masters, walled off from their subjects behind fortress walls, a centre of power designed and conceived to be the heart of the world itself, an axis about which the entire universe was expected to revolve.

# 4

# The Forbidden City: 1368–1644

T HERE IS A LONG WALK to his mausoleum. The subway station is some 42km from the centre of town, and even then its name is Scenic Area for the Thirteen Tombs (*Shisan Ling Jingqu*). The visitor passes through several gates, and along a 7km road lined with statues of mighty beasts, scowling warriors and loyal scholars. The Thirteen Tombs stretch out in a semicircle in the foothills of the mountains to the north, a spread of temples with yellow, imperial roofs, each set in maroon-walled enclosures like miniature versions of the Forbidden City.

His mausoleum is directly ahead of the approach road – every tomb has a Sacred Way approaching it, but you have just walked along the longest, for the greatest of the Ming emperors.

Yongle, the Emperor of Perpetual Happiness (1360–1424), was the third of the Ming emperors, but the first to be buried in Beijing, his adopted capital. His bronze effigy dominates the main hall of his necropolis (see Gazetteer: Further Afield), seemingly in imitation of the throne he once occupied. He is thick-set, bearded, sitting with legs confidently wide apart, his hands resting on his thighs as if just about to issue a sternly worded decree. There is naked power coiled here, simmering in the air. His title is something of a misnomer; he was not happy with simply being a prince. He took the throne for himself, and moved his capital all the way north, dragging China's fortunes with it, for much of the next 600 years.

## Perpetual Happiness

The generation of warfare that led to the establishment of the Ming dynasty did considerable damage to Khanbalikh. The city had grown so large under the Mongols that it was unable to support itself without a stable country to keep its population fed. With the Grand Canal damaged by floods, silt and neglect, many in Khanbalikh had starved. The city's outlying regions were abandoned during the strife and plague; the old Mongol aristocrats were dead or exiled, and few Chinese seemed willing to seek out a place whose importance rested on now-discredited contacts with the peoples of the north and west. China's focus began to shift southward once more – Nanjing was now the capital, with Kaifeng in the west a subsidiary administrative hub.

Nanjing sat at the centre of rich and fertile plains, on a *real* river that was navigable far upstream – it needed none of the artificial watercourses or unstable supply routes of Khanbalikh. Its situation would allow it to grow much larger, and its location kept the new government closely linked to the loyal south, not the untrustworthy north.

With propagandist zeal and a smidgen of superstition, the old north capital was renamed Beiping, 'Northern Peace', seemingly in the hope that harmony would prevail in the old Mongol heartland. Nor was the newly christened Northern Peace expected to fall into ruins. It was still a regional capital, and soon gained a princely patron whose influence would radically change the city's fortunes.

The first emperor of the Ming had 26 sons, most of whom were appointed as regional governors. Only the eldest was kept in the new capital; the rest were scattered across the empire and tasked with maintaining order in their father's name. The emperor's fourth son was given the northeast as his princedom, adopting the archaic title of Prince of Yan, in honour of the region's ancient past as the Land of Swallows. In the midst of empire-wide rebuilding and reconstruction, the newly arrived prince oversaw radical remodelling in the old Mongol capital.

Initially, he had no interest in restoring the city to its full glory. The canal was left derelict, and many of the old Yuan palaces were pulled down. The imperial city itself was reduced in size, its north wall moved southward, to create a more modest and manageable private area. Many of the old Mongol gardens were retained, but Coal Hill to the north now stood outside the imperial citadel proper.

Even though Chinese civilisation had supposedly been restored, it was impossible to expect a century of foreign rule to have left no mark. In the case of the Prince of Yan, growing up in a Mongol-ruled society seemed to impart certain expectations about the succession.

With the death of his elder brother, the Prince of Yan began to assert that he, and not his young nephew, should be recognised as the rightful heir to the Ming emperor. It was a decidedly Mongol attitude towards the imperial succession, and one that the emperor was not prepared to allow. When he eventually died in 1398, he expressly ordered his many surviving sons to stay away from the enthronement of his heir in Nanjing, for fear that they would attempt a coup.

Despite these admonitions, the Prince of Yan set out for Nanjing anyway, and was only thwarted when the army blocked his path. He returned, embarrassed, to the north, but the damage was already done. The Prince of Yan and his nephew would fight over the future of the empire in a three-year civil war, which ended with Nanjing in ruins, the nephew nowhere to be found, and the administrative centre of the empire moved back north to the Prince of Yan's power-base. Beijing had become the capital of all China, and would remain so until the present day, except for a brief period in the 20th century.

The Prince of Yan, remembered in the dynastic histories as Yongle, the Emperor of Perpetual Happiness, was thus responsible for the rehabilitation of Beijing as an imperial capital, not only through his early reconstruction, but also for even more extensive rebuilding undertaken after his victory. It is said that Yongle stayed in the Beijing region out of a sense of military zeal – the hated Mongols were still at large, and he intended to personally lead the mop-up operations against them. But Beijing was also his personal fiefdom, and the place where he was most likely to feel safe. There may have been Mongol enemies to the north, but Yongle cannot have placed much trust in his many disgruntled brothers or their expanding families in the south.

## The Living God of Wealth

From 1406 to 1420, Beijing was a building site once more; its palaces renovated, its lakes dredged and the grandeur of its Grand Canal restored. The Emperor of Perpetual Happiness faced strong resistance from his engineers; many regarded the city as a doomed venture. Yongle's own Minister of Works dared to refuse the commission, reminding his ruler that the region was still widely regarded as the Waste of the Bitter Sea, and that the dragons of the area were too powerful to overcome. By 'dragons', the minister is likely to have meant the many unfavourable features of the terrain, but, to a casual reader, some of the court documents regarding the reconstruction can often seem as if Yongle was ordering his engineers to do battle with serpents and savage beasts.

The two imperial officers charged with redeveloping Beijing were legendarily at odds. Whether this is historically accurate or mere dramatic licence is unclear, but city folklore maintains that they sulked in separate quarters, each determined to prove the other to be a fool, only to be united in their town planning when both received the same vision – the ghost of a young boy, supposedly the spirit of Nezha himself, demigod of past dynasties, the suicidal multi-limbed child-hero who supposedly rode on fiery wheels and terrorised the local dragons. Nezha instructed each of them to 'copy' his own body. It is, so popular legend claims, this imitation of the eight-armed figure of Nezha that caused Beijing to have its Ming dynasty layout.

Even when one has a Ming dynasty city map, and not a later Qing-, Republican- or Communist-era street plan, the idea that the city is laid out in the shape of a giant god seems ludicrous. Geomancers have attempted lengthy discourses on the meaning of Beijing as a recumbent god, suggesting that a certain gate is an ear of Nezha; a certain pair of wells are his eyes; his feet rest on a pair of temples to the south; or that the space in front of the Gate of Heavenly Peace is his lungs. And since someone inevitably asks, his penis is thought to be the bridge that leads south from the Rear Gate. Even before the modern era, local inhabitants regarded such superstition with mild embarrassment, and not even the *feng shui* masters seemed to take it all that seriously. It is not the image of a god in Beijing's town planning that concerns the Chinese, it is the implication that however the city was designed, a substantial element of its origin lay not in human artifice, but in divine inspiration.

The Ming-era reconstruction of Beijing comes accompanied by many other folktales, from merry anecdotes of supernatural assistance, to macabre tales of the grotesque. Yongle initiated an incentive scheme to encourage outlying provinces to aid the project – a decision which led to legends about the reconstruction of Beijing to spring up far from its actual location. In one case, it was said that the distant mountain of *Shenmu* ('Sacred Trees') gained its name for the speed with which timber from the region had been floated down the Yangtze River, ready for shipment north to Beijing.

Since the Mongols left the city in a hurry, it was not a surprise that they left much of their possessions behind. Stories of Yongle's men pulling down Mongol palaces seem only partly born out from memories of demolition and renovation. Officers of the new regime were also likely to have been on the lookout for buried treasure, squirreled away by the departed dynasty.

Folklore soon intervened, and the simple hunt for concealed bullion took on a legendary status, with stories of a man called the Living God of Wealth, blessed, or rather, cursed with the ability to find buried treasure. According to legend, the Living God of Wealth was an ordinary man with an extraordinary gift – somehow, he was able to simply know where valuable objects could be found. But after years of abuse from greedy bullies, he had taken on a hermit's existence, refusing to profit from his own knowledge, and choosing to live as a pauper.

It is likely that the story of a dirty, wretched tramp dragged before Ming officers and ordered to lead them to riches contains within it a more tragic tale – that of a loyal servant of the old regime, abandoned by his former masters and tortured by a new order hungry for monetary gain. Yongle ordered them to beat him until he took them to the treasure, and to beat him all the more if he turned out to be bluffing.

Before long, the bleeding, pleading form of the Living God of Wealth brought his tormentors to a patch of waste ground, and told them to dig. Beneath the surface they found ten secret vaults, containing nearly half a billion *taels* of silver. This, we are told, is the origin of the strangely named Ten Vaults Lake (*Shichahai*), which formed when the great hole in the ground eventually filled up with water. This folkloric explanation conveniently forgets that the lake had already been in the area for centuries – Shichahai, moreover, is more liable to derive its name from a corruption of 'Tens of Shrines', in recognition of the number of places of worship in the area.

But even as the brutality of the takeover crushed and beat down the last remnants of the old regime, the new Ming dynasty began to build new ministries and public works. One exception was the Mongol-era sewage and drainage system, which was left derelict. For the next few centuries, the removal of night-soil was outsourced to carters who would collect it every day, in order to dry and sell as fertiliser on the surrounding fields. As so often happens in Chinese society, human labour was found to be a cheaper and more efficient means of dealing with a problem than modern technology, not the least because one man's waste was another man's commodity. This, however, was also the beginning of Ming- and Qing-era Beijing's reputation for smelling awful.

## The Centre of the World

Shielding all but the tallest buildings or hilltops from the outside world, the Ming-era city walls remained a defining part of the image of Beijing right up until the time they were demolished in the 20th century. As late as 1922, the former US ambassador Paul Reinsch could write:

> The towers and city walls of Peking, an impressive and astounding apparition of strength and permanence, befit this scene. Solemn and mysterious, memorable for their size, extent and general inevitableness of structure, they can be compared only with the Pyramids, or with great mountains fashioned by the hand of Nature herself.

Down on what was once the southeast corner of the city wall, the shiny glass towers of the Central Business District loom above carefully tended grass verges. The area has the icy, corporate elegance of business districts in American cities – the roads are wide, the sidewalks empty but for street sweepers, the lush grasses well-tended but only for show – regular lawn grass does not flourish in parched north China, and is usually replaced with a tough, sharp-bladed facsimile. One could almost believe one were in Atlanta, were it not for the great stone building that sits at the corner of two main roads like a medieval castle, its thick walls crenellated to protect archers from attack, its roof dotted with the distinctive silhouettes of astronomical instruments – a giant metal sextant, a quadrant, an altazimuth and an armillary sphere.

The Imperial Observatory was originally set up by Khubilai Khan at a different address, but was moved to its current location at the beginning of the Ming dynasty, during one of the city's greatest periods of renovation. It looks like a fortress because that's what it was – it is one of the last remaining pieces of the old city wall, left intact because of its additional function, while other sections were pulled down and moved further out as part of the city's expansion.

'The scientific instruments to be seen there are admirable,' wrote Victor Meignan in 1885. 'They are made of bronze, supported on feet of the same metal, in which all the fancies of Chinese art have been lavished. The contortions of these mountings, composed of dragons and grotesque monsters, produce a striking contrast to the regular forms of the spheres, the parallel lines and astronomical figures which they sustain at great height in the air.'

Many locals don't know what the building is. Modern slang has truncated its name until it is often dismissed as the 'old observation tower'. One can occasionally find Beijing trainspotters on its battlements, peering down at the approach to the nearby railway station. It seems that for many taxi drivers and passers-by, it is these anorakked figures that are the 'observers'.

The historical truth is even more surprising. The Imperial Observatory was a vital part of the Chinese world order. The superstitions of court religion demanded precise calculations for planning auspicious events. The portents had to be precisely right for the dating of a coronation or a royal wedding; government appointments needed to be timed to gain the maximum good fortune. Important decisions and journeys had to be postponed until the precise time that the fates would give them the greatest chance for success. In order to keep tabs on these many factors in the Chinese calendar, the Imperial Observatory was responsible for the planning of almanacs and astronomical tables. At first the imperial astronomers were locals; then, in the time of Khubilai Khan, many were Muslims.

During the later Ming dynasty, the observatory became the site of quarrelling foreign factions, as the Chinese and Arab astronomers fought to discredit new arrivals from Europe. The Jesuits, of course, hoped to convert the Chinese to Christianity, but planned on playing a long game by first making themselves and their scientific knowledge indispensable. The Jesuits had more accurate equipment than their counterparts, and soon ruled the roost when it came to organising the calendar.

Since the earliest times, when unrest in the Land of Swallows was tracked through the appearances of meteors and comets in the corresponding sector of the sky, the Chinese had believed that the constellations reflect and influence earthly events. But if Beijing were the centre of the world Under Heaven, and Beijing's ruler its paramount being, then the rules of propriety demanded that Beijing's centre had a constellation of its own – a central citadel that represented the very axis about which the universe would turn.

Confucius said: 'Ruling by moral example will make you like the Pole Star, which remains firm in place while the other stars revolve around it.' If heaven were a map of earth, then the centre of the world would need to be an earthly analogue of the pole star itself, which was popularly believed by Chinese stargazers to have a purple tint. For this reason, the private citadel at the centre of Beijing, prohibited to commoners for centuries, was known as the 'Purple Forbidden City'. The universe, it was expected, would turn around it, in harmony and awe.

The best time to visit the Forbidden City is off-season, in the dead of winter, when flurries of snow have chased away the tour groups. On a spring day, the early morning crowds are out in force, whisking briskly around the Centre of the Universe in a couple of hours, so the one- and two-day parties can be hurtling down the road in a bus to see the Great Wall before the evening's duck dinner.

The halls tower above the visitor, on stepped ziggurats of marble and alabaster. Draconic gargoyles spit water into the gutters, and great bronze cauldrons sit before each palace – leftovers from the days when the buildings were mostly wooden, and the eunuchs needed a ready source to extinguish localised fires. The tiles beneath my feet are worn down like the flagstones of the Marco Polo Bridge, but not from centuries of attrition. This damage has been done in mere decades, by millions of tramping feet, as armies of tourists roam the main thoroughfares that were once the sole domain of the imperial household. The flagstones are regularly replaced, as are the palaces themselves, renovated in permanent rotation. Some have glassed facades, permitting views of shadowy interiors stacked with dusty memorabilia of the imperial era. Others have been fitted with turnstile gates, hoping to relieve the visitor of a few more coins for that little bit extra – an exhibition of royal jewellery, perhaps, or some *objets d'art* from a particular reign.

In the shadow of the great halls there are smaller buildings used in the past by government officers. Here, there is a building where the military had their quartermaster. Here is another where young princes received their schooling.

The approach to the Hall of Preserving Harmony, like many other imperial buildings, features twin staircases, separated by a carved alabaster image of dragons twirling through clouds. The strange design is a stirring relic of the imperial era – the space between the staircases is decorated because it would never be walked upon. Instead, the emperor was borne up the stairs in his litter. He would float above the dragon images in his chair, while his litter-bearers trudged up the steps either side. In the northern sector are the private apartments of the imperial family, surrounded by carefully landscaped gardens, scattered with pavilions and teahouses. These days, there is also a display of numerous funny-shaped rocks, presented to the emperor as birthday presents. He would probably have preferred socks.

These days, it is known locally as the 'old palace' (*Gu Gong*). It is a mandatory inclusion for the tourist, somewhat to its detriment, since its sheer size and the weight of its story can over-awe the unprepared visitor. For many foreigners, the Forbidden City soon leads to the common condition of feeling 'templed out'. Its side passages are a maze of anonymous russet walls, its gardens an identikit of intricate but nameless buildings. The greatest service done for the site was by Bernardo Bertolucci, whose 1987 movie *The Last Emperor* helped untold millions of foreigners appreciate the Forbidden City in context.

But this is the place where *The Last Emperor* happened. Not merely the location for the Bertolucci film, but the actual place where 'Henry' Puyi, final Lord of Ten Thousand Years, once frightened the eunuchs by riding on a bicycle. Within the complex, by the ubiquitous postcard sellers, behind the cash machine, is the place where a terrifying Manchu general turned on the steps to address a crowd, announcing that he would be taking over, against the background of a smouldering palace building.

The Forbidden City was the centrepiece of Ming- and Qing-era Beijing. Much of what remains today is more recent, from the Ming's Qing usurpers, but even so, the basic design has been retained, a recreation of the ancient idea of the centre of the perfect city, at the centre of the perfect world, presided over by the perfect ruler.

Beyond the walls of the Forbidden City, Ming-era Beijing struggled to live up to the architectural plan. Rivers and lakes unhelpfully broke up some of the straight-line streets. The expansion of the outer walls of the city north, creating a suburb that would have completely surrounded the Forbidden City, was never completed, forcing the idealised urban design to fall a little short of the Yongle Emperor's ambitions.

That old favourite, the family of dragons was soon back in local myth, sneaking into town in human form to suck wells dry. They were defeated at last by the architect Liu Bowen, who successfully arranged for the diversion of the waters from a nearby river. One legend tells of a stone mason working on the Beijing project, who thought he saw the dragons making off with the water and gave chase, only to be lured into a dry river bed just before the floodgates were opened, bringing a fatal torrent crashing down upon him. To hear the story told, it seems suspiciously close to an old tale of a sacrifice to a river god.

But Beijing's water supply remains salty and faintly unpleasant – said to be the dragons' last revenge, hoarding all the good water at the Jade Spring in the hills, and leaving Beijing with nothing but the dregs. For the residents of the imperial citadel, the dragons were thwarted by a daily convoy of carts that rolled into the hills to the Jade Spring, stocked up with fresh water, and then brought it back to the palace. In the evenings, they would be replaced by the sewage-bearing 'honey-wagons' heading out of the city with a very different cargo. Occasionally, exploratory wells would happen upon better supplies inside the city, and wealthy locals would soon buy up the daily supply, such as in Wangfujing, the 'Well of the Prince'. Geomancers attempted to read some sort of pattern into the occasional discovery, claiming that the sites of good wells in Ming dynasty Beijing followed the shape of a giant centipede, sent to burrow into the earth by a sorcerer who was tired of the bitter taste of Beijing tea.

The unnamed wizard was not the only supernatural assistant. A story about the strangely ornate watchtowers of the Forbidden City claims that Yongle ordered his masons to come up with something distinctive on pain of death, and then left them to it. After three months of deliberation (notably, the same deadline given to Khubilai's bell-makers in Mongol times), the builders were running out of patience and hope, and one of the carpenters went outside to get some air. There, he bumped into an aged pedlar who sold him an elaborate cricket cage. Back in the meeting room, the carpenter showed it to his fellow workers, who marvelled at the construction that somehow used nine beams and eighteen pillars to create a roof with seventy-two ridges. The builders copied the cricket cage for the construction of the watchtowers, and later folklore suggested that the cricket seller had really been the God of Carpenters in disguise.

But much of the folklore about the Forbidden City relates to its outer courts – those parts, such as the watchtowers, that could be glimpsed by the commoners. There is a fascination for the historian in being able to stand in the places that centuries of people could only read about in dynastic chronicles – the inner chambers where empresses watched acrobats, or the well where a concubine was murdered, or committed suicide, depending on whom one believes. The Forbidden City is a place to be savoured over many visits, coupled with reading and appreciation of the many historical moments it has witnessed. The half-day allotted to so many tour groups seems like a pointless exercise – a perplexing parade of names and dates, delivered amid big open spaces, and occasional glimpses into dark rooms. One first visits the Forbidden City out of a sense of duty. Its true majesty and wondrous history takes a lifetime to appreciate.

Although he is remembered as the architect of Ming Beijing, Yongle did not flourish in his new capital. The paint was barely dry on the new Forbidden City when it became the home to scandal. Beijing might have represented a new start for the Ming dynasty, but despite being far removed from the old capitals in the south, it spontaneously developed troubles of its own.

Southern Chinese beauties, those capricious, wilful creatures that had brought down many an emperor in past centuries, were in short supply in Beijing. But that did not seem to bother Yongle – in fact, his particular fetish seems to have been for foreign girls, particularly Koreans from just over the border. One such concubine, Lady Quan, died soon after Yongle's return from a campaign, and was later found to have been poisoned by a rival, who had arranged for arsenic to be dropped into the poor girl's tea. The matter only came to light several years later as part of palace feud between two other Koreans, when a girl from a poor background accused a snooty palace rival of being the poisoner.

The alleged poisoner was branded and died 'soon afterwards' – an indicator of suicide, enforced or voluntary. The accuser fared little better, since she later hanged herself, afraid that a platonic relationship with a palace eunuch might be regarded as a betrayal of her imperial master. Yongle, however, refused to believe this explanation, and tortured the dead lady's servants until they 'confessed' that she had killed herself because she was afraid the emperor would discover she was planning to assassinate him.

The allegation led to a savage purge of palace women, with over two thousand eventually implicated and tortured to death. The real truth came out in the dying curse of one of the victims, who alleged that Yongle was impotent. Beijing life had given him terrible rheumatism, and left him unable to carry out his conjugal duties. This had left his many dozens of concubines and wives with perilously little to do, and turned them all upon each other.

## The Eight Great Sights

With such bad omens, it is perhaps not a surprise that the Chinese began to suspect that their almanacs might be in error. Yongle's successors kept careful tabs on matters of state *feng shui*, questioning many of his city planning decisions. The temple complex to Heaven and Earth he had built in the southern suburbs was radically remodelled. One of its most distinctive buildings, the multi-eaved circular Hall of Prayer for Good Harvests (today simply called the Temple of Heaven) has become one of the most recognisable buildings in Beijing, although the version that exists today is relatively recent. The Ming dynasty original was struck by lightning and burned to the ground in 1889, although the modern building is supposedly a reasonable facsimile. Not that Victor Meignan's account of it in 1885 is liable to lead to a flood of visitors.

> I shall say little of the Temple of Heaven and the Temple of Agriculture, because they are not interesting. The first especially is unworthy of the exalted name it bears. It is an immense park surrounded with walls, in which chapels and pretty pavilions, covered with blue porcelain, are distributed, and where a subdued light penetrates through blinds composed of little tubes of blue glass placed parallel. A platform of white marble is raised in the middle of the park, and it is here the Emperor occasionally comes to offer with his own hand sacrifices to the Divinity.

After 1534, when Earth-worship was moved to a new, more geomantically appropriate location, the complex was given over entirely to the worship of Heaven, and still has its remarkable circular multi-tiered altar. For many centuries, this was the location of one of the most important ceremonies of the imperial calendar. On the day before the Winter Solstice, the emperors of the Ming and Qing dynasties would leave the Forbidden City in a great procession that nobody would see – the people of Beijing were ordered to remain indoors on pain of death, while the religious procession marched on a road strewn with yellow dust, toward the great Altar of Heaven. The ceremony began before dawn, involving parties of carefully coordinated 'temple dancers' on the lower tiers of the site. The emperor himself, however, was left alone at the pinnacle of the altar, standing before symbolic offerings to the spirits and his ancestors, while his herald read out his prayers, his respects and an annual report of events and accomplishments in the empire. The ceremony would finish with the ceremonial burning of sacrificial offerings, in a series of braziers that flanked the altar, each leading to a great tiled sacrificial oven.

Yongle's workers also radically rebuilt the Mongol walls, which seem to have been largely comprised of rammed earth, and subject to decay and erosion if left untended. The Ming builders faced the earthen ramparts with bricks, or in some cases, built completely new walls within the perimeter of the old ones – the depopulation of the plague period left the former Khan's City not requiring anything near the land area of its heyday.

Wall building also went on outside the city, to legendary effect. The most visible achievement of Yongle's dynasty, begun in his life-time but not completed until decades later, was the most famous monument of all in China, the Great Wall. The Ming wall was not the first to mark out the northern border of China, but it was a much more enduring undertaking than its predecessors. Whereas previous 'great walls', dating back to the time of the First Emperor, had utilised rammed earth, wooden palisades and ditches, the Ming wall was a sturdy bricks-and-mortar affair. Earlier walls had often been used less as border markers, and more as bases from which Chinese troops and colonists could sally forth against the enemies of the north and west. Yongle's wall had a genuine defensive role, with construction commencing in recognition of a new policy towards the Mongols. Unable to hound China's former rulers to a final defeat in their homeland, the Ming dynasty instead hoped to wall them off, out of sight and mind.

Despite Yongle's successors defining the northern border of China with iconic finality, there were soon Chinese colonists to the north of it. Ironically, it was their relationship with the Manchu people to the north that encouraged the Manchus to consider ruling China for themselves. When the Ming dynasty eventually fell, Chinese colonists from north of the wall, who had gone just native enough to serve new masters, would fill many critical roles in the invading forces.

Today, much of the Great Wall remains in ruins, although several portions have been painstakingly restored to its Ming-era glory. US president Richard Nixon became one of the first high-profile foreign visitors to the restored section, apocryphally proclaiming: 'It sure is a great wall.' In the decades that have followed, the Great Wall has become an industry of its own, and the Badaling section that Nixon saw has become something of a tourist trap. It is close enough to Beijing that a tour bus can take in both Badaling and the Ming tombs in one day, meaning that although the wall is supposedly thousands of miles long, its sections nearest Beijing are crawling with people.

Recent years have seen other sections restored, with decisions based largely on either transport access or the opportunity offered for an impressive backdrop. Broken-down sections first attract tourists off the beaten track, then the inevitable hawkers, then the renovators and safety consultants who often strip away much of the historical charm along with the dangers. Today, one must drive for several hours to find a relatively deserted section of the Great Wall, and visitors are encouraged not to – far better, for all concerned, that they are corralled into areas with handrails, public transport access, and a restaurant.

Standing on the Great Wall is a beautiful and terrifying experience. It still has the same effect on modern visitors that it was designed to have on the Mongols. Stretching away as far as the eye can see, across mountains and valleys until it peters out on the horizon, only to lurch back into view again as it rings a strategic site a few miles further over, the Great Wall still sends a message to any who see it. *This is what China can do*, it says. *Not just to you, but to ourselves* – not for nothing did earlier defensive projects gain the wall the nickname of 'the Longest Cemetery'. The Great Wall is a testament to the millions that died to build it, and a symbol of fortress China.

Yongle also laid the earliest foundations of Beijing's tourist industry, by commanding his ministers to come up with a list of peerless attractions that could be promoted as the Eight Great Sights of Beijing. His reasoning was political, aimed not at encouraging vacationing visitors, but at whipping up a sense of local heritage. Yongle still faced unsteady support in the south, and his Eight Great Sights project was designed to encourage poems, songs and prose to establish Beijing's image as a true capital, and hence his own as the rightful ruler. These eight wonders of Beijing, as chronicled in the early Ming dynasty, are a dreary collection of half-hearted seasonal slogans, sounding precisely like the kind of nonsense one might get in a new town without many old or famous landmarks, from a committee who could not be bothered to look too far from their office window.

The Marco Polo Bridge, still standing after many centuries, was dragged in as one of the exhibits, notably because it had cropped up in a poem from one of the emperors of the Jin dynasty. What was good enough for the Khitans was good enough for the Ming: the moon at dawn on the Marco Polo Bridge. The Great Wall was also a mandatory inclusion, although the feature chosen was not technically part of the Wall proper, but an isolated fortress on a mountain pass, tarted up with an irrelevant spot of nature promotion to become one of the Eight Sights: the lush greenery around the fortress at Juyong Pass. The committee followed up with the sun on the Golden Terrace (a site that is no longer extant). Seeing a pattern that might do their selection for them, they scrabbled around for more elements and opposites. The trees around the old ruined entrance to the ancient capital, the Thistle Gate – they might do. But since there was already a mention of greenery, the committee added that the sight was only 'great' when the forest was viewed in the mist.

There were pretty rainbows out in the hills; in the mists where the Jade Spring of fresh water bubbled to the surface... they heard. Snow looked good on the Western Hills... sometimes. In spring, it was often pleasantly warm on Hortensia Island... apparently. The ripples on the water, the committee decided, looked nice in Beihai Park. And that was the eight, done – conspicuously with a couple being visible from the same spot, as if someone had dashed off the last two as an afterthought on his way to work.

## The Advent of the Manchus

The desire to keep Beijing as the capital, and to maintain relations with the peoples even further north, risked recreating the old north-south divide. Far to the south, Nanjing was kept as a sleepy alternate-capital, its ministers and officials diligently shadowing the functions of the true centre, just in case Beijing should have to be abandoned. Even as the campaigns against the Mongols petered out, and the Ming mindset became more about hiding behind walls than proactively pursuing new frontiers, the Ming people continued to intermix across the border.

Nanjing, as it would eventually turn out, was not the only place that was shadowing Beijing. North of the Great Wall, the people of Manchuria were developing a love, respect and covetousness towards the power and wealth of the Ming dynasty. In their own capital of Mukden (modern Shenyang), the Manchus began to formulate ministries and offices designed to copy and eventually surpass those of the Chinese in Beijing. Eventually, the ruling clan of the Manchus proclaimed a new decree – that the Ming dynasty was fated to fall, and that it was the destiny of the Manchus to replace it. Just as Khubilai Khan had proclaimed the foundation of his Yuan dynasty several years before conquering China, the Manchus proclaimed their own replacement for the Ming somewhat in advance of their actual rule. At first, they called it the Jin (Golden) dynasty in imitation of their Jurchen cousins of old.

In China, the Ming dynasty staggered and stumbled, barely able to pay the troops who staffed the Great Wall. Bad weather led to bad harvests, in turn creating famine and disease. The general Wu Sangui, charged with holding back the northern barbarians, held his army together with charisma and promises, until the fateful day when he switched sides.

Dwindling finances on the Wall were not the only sign of trouble. Rebellions in the hinterland offered still more worries to the fretful Ming dynasty. Even as thousands of Ming soldiers stared north from the battlements of the Great Wall, Beijing fell to a Chinese rebel. Li Zicheng, a former postman, had led a bandit existence for several years before leading his forces to the gates of Beijing itself. The city fell swiftly – its troops demoralised, its cannons without ammunition, it defences compromised by years of neglect and corruption.

At the Great Wall, the Ming general Wu Sangui chose a new and deadly alliance, inviting the Manchus to accompany him in a mission to relieve the capital. They never left.

A great battle in a sandstorm was fought at Shahe (Sandy River), now a station on the Changping subway line. Travel by car or bus to Badaling to see the Great Wall, and you are sure to pass it, marked by a huge statue of Li Zicheng on horseback at the off-ramp for the Ming Tombs. The People's Republic of China chooses to commemorate him, the commoner who overthrew an empire for a scant few weeks, rather than the Ming general who made a fateful, Faustian pact to destroy him. As for the Manchu hordes who accompanied Wu Sangui through the wall and into Beijing, their monuments are all around you.

# 5

# 'Peking': 1644–1912

For a moment, I am alone in the chamber. The walls are painted in the bright red of marital bliss. The screen in front of me is painted with a giant pattern comprising conjoined *xi* ('happiness'), a traditional nuptial decoration. This quiet, deserted hall looks much like any other to the average Western visitor, particularly on a day trip to the Forbidden City, where one big bare room in a big red hall can often end up looking very much like another. But there is something special about this place, with its double-happiness on the wall, and the entwined dragon and phoenix designs repeated on the furniture. The lanterns similarly bear a double-*xi* design. This quiet hall, this very room, is a place of bridal celebration. Three different Qing emperors spent their wedding nights here. They drank wine with their new brides on this very bed. There is joy in this room, but also nervousness, and pathos. Of the three emperors, two of them died young in suspicious circumstances, the victims of a palace conspiracy by old widows determined to cling to power. The silence is remarkable, as is the chill – even though it is a warm sunny day outside, I see a cloud of my breath in the air.

The haunting silence is broken by an ear-splitting mechanical shriek – a handheld loudhailer that has a built-in tune. At the touch of a button, it blares the first few bars of the *Laurel and Hardy* theme, at a decibel level twice that of the average ice cream van. It is in the hands of an earnest Chinese guide, who has used it to shock a group of Italian tourists into stunned silence.

'THIS IS THE HALL OF EARTHLY TRANQUILITY!' she yells into her megaphone. 'FORMER RESIDENCE OF THE EMPRESSES, AND A PLACE OF SILENT CONTEMPLATION!'

## A Square Atop a Rectangle

Although history books usually show a tidy single date for the regime change, the fall of Beijing to the Manchus in 1644 did not bring the rest of China immediately with it. A resistance movement continued for another generation, until the last rebels either forgot what they were fighting for or faded into organisations indistinguishable from criminal gangs. In an unguarded moment at a banquet, one Manchu nobleman claimed that his people originally had little expectation of taking China south of the Yellow River. Instead, they had set their sights on seizing the northern territory once held by the Khitans and Jurchen, but had been startled by the lack of true Ming resistance, and by the numbers of Chinese subjects willing to join their cause. As a result, in the early days of the Qing dynasty, the Manchus did not have much time for rebuilding. The surviving buildings of the old Ming Forbidden City were simply repurposed for the new owners, with little more than a change in signposts and the occasional lick of paint. It took many years before Qing-era buildings began to replace those of the departed dynasty in the centre of Beijing.

Qing-era Beijing long retained a sense of being an occupied terri-tory. It was divided into two walled cities, a square atop a rectangle. The 'Manchu' city, whose walls are now traced by the path of Line 2 of the Subway, was home to the conquerors. A smaller, 'Chinese' city stretched from what is now the bottom corner of Tiananmen Square, several city blocks to what is now the southern edge of the Second Ring Road – this, too, follows the outline of the old city. Of its towering, crenelated walls, little trace survives today, except for the vestigial names of long-gone gates, and a small stretch left stand-ing in the southeast corner of the Manchu town, near what is now Beijing railway station.

The fall of the Ming dynasty created a number of villains for Chinese history, on every side of the conflict. The last Ming emper-ors were painted as unworthy successors to the noble Chinese who ousted the Mongols, failing their subjects and their ancestors by losing the support of Heaven once more. Wu Sangui is a classically tragic figure in Chinese drama – a soldier torn between his allegiance to a doomed dynasty, temptations on offer from devilish invaders, and a desire for revenge against the usurper who has killed his father and raped his lover. Only Li Zicheng has gained some form of reha-bilitation. In the Communist era, he was lionised for his role in toppling the old imperial order, and for attracting humble farmers to his standard, eventually becoming the subject of an influential 1963 historical novel by Yao Xueyin (sadly untranslated).

The Manchus ruled China during a tumultuous period in which geography no longer kept it out of contact with other powers. Ironically, Beijing was more isolated than its own periphery, far to the north, walled in by desert and mountains, and with a sea port in Tianjin that was iced up from November to March every year. During the Age of Exploration, as the Portuguese and Spanish were rounding Africa and mapping the Americas, the Chinese stayed put. In the earliest days of the Ming dynasty, Chinese embassies had sailed as far as Madagascar, but the great age of Chinese exploration was soon brought to an end. Finances dwindled, the Ming emperors had other problems on their minds, and besides, it was thought unseemly that imperial embassies would go in search of recognition of their own greatness from foreigners – far better that the barbarians approach China themselves, with the correct degree of etiquette, and a fair amount of fear and trembling. Beijing itself may have played some part in this – the landlocked capital, forever clinging to its inland canal routes and its camel trains across the plains, may have encouraged a landlubber attitude in its ruling class. Whereas Chinese in the south, in the great river port of Nanjing or the seafaring towns of Fuzhou or Canton, had long traditions of maritime trade, the northern Chinese preferred to look inwards, at the great sea of grassland that extended to the west, or the parched, dusty deserts of the hinterland.

The Manchus were even more landlocked than the Ming dynasty. With a nomadic background and a love of horsemanship and the steppe life, the Manchu ruling house was pathologically afraid of the sea. In the 17th century, they briefly ordered the complete depopulation of the seacoast to a distance of some thirty miles, hoping to cut China off completely from the undue influence of the coastline. Instead of building a navy, the Manchus briefly attempted to push the sea itself out of mind, creating a swathe of barren territory more than a day's march across, patrolled only by government troops with orders to kill any loiterers on sight.

With such an attitude, it is perhaps not surprising that the Manchus were taken by surprise by the arrival of the European nations in the Far East.

Beijing's northern location played a part in China's decline during the 18th and 19th century. Contact with European powers was initially limited to the far south of the Chinese continent, through the port of Canton. Europeans pushed for further trading opportunities and contacts inland, but Beijing remained largely unimpressed by their requests and entreaties, and unaware of their urgency. Arguably, the protocols and politesse of Chinese government communiqués, in continuing to bow and scrape before the emperor's majesty, misled him as to the seriousness of the situation.

The aging British ambassador George (later Lord) Macartney arrived in China in 1793, hoping to establish diplomatic relations. Instead, he scandalised the Manchu court by refusing to kow-tow before the Qianlong Emperor, and by looking down his nose at a valuable gift of jade. Meanwhile, the emperor was baffled by Macartney's entreaties; China was the Centre of the World, and prided itself on needing nothing from barbarian neighbours. The concept of 'trade' was entirely beyond the emperor, who advised Macartney: 'You... should simply act in conformity with Our wishes by strengthening your loyalty and swearing perpetual obedience, so as to ensure that your country may share the blessings of peace.'

## Lanes and Alleys

Macartney left a record of the few days that he spent in Beijing that October, writing that the city was 'one of the largest in the world, and justly to be admired for its walls and gates, the distribution of its quarters, the width and allineation [sic] of its streets, the grandeur of its triumphal arches and the number and magnificence of its palaces'. The city that Macartney saw still bore reminders that the Manchus were conquerors – policing was 'singularly strict', and Macartney was surprised by a curfew that effectively shut down every main street, 'shut up by barricades at each end and a guard... constantly patrolling'. He was also taken aback by the population's close-packed living arrangements.

> [A]t Pekin one scarcely meets with any but men, as the women seldom stir abroad. The houses... are very closely inhabited, it being no uncommon thing for a dozen people to be crowded into one small chamber that in England would be considered as a scanty accommodation for a single person... None of the streets are paved so that in wet weather they are covered in mud and in dry weather the dust is excessively disagreeable pervading

every place and every thing, but what renders it intolerably offensive is the stench.

The city retained the 'chess-board' design of wide thoroughfares as mentioned by Marco Polo, and within each square was a maze of small alleys and tracks. Strictly speaking, a street that runs east-west is called a *hutong* ('alley') while one that runs north-south is called a *xiang* ('lane'). The terms had been in use since the Han dynasty, but have come to be associated with the Manchu period, not the least because the word for 'well' in Manchu, *huttog*, sounded similar, and led many historians to assume in error that such architecture began with the Manchu conquest. They remained an integral part of Beijing life well into the 20th century, as recalled by Ellen LaMotte in 1916:

> You wind your way along a narrow, unpaved street, or *hutong* – a street full of little open-air shops, cook-shops, stalls of various kinds, and then come upon a high, blank wall with a pair of stone lions at the gateway and an enormous red lacquer gate, heavily barred, and that's your house. The gateman opens to your ring, and as the big doors swing back, you see nothing of the courtyard... you are confronted by the devil screen, a high stone wall [that]... blocks the evil spirits that fly in when the compound gates are opened – the blind evil spirits, that can only fly in straight paths, and hence crash against the devil screen when they enter.

In fact the *hutongs* represent the most traditional form of Chinese architecture imaginable, comprising multiple clusters of *siheyuan* ('quadrangles') – small, walled courtyards with long, low houses running right around their walls, but for the opening afforded by a central gate. The main reason that women 'seldom stirred abroad' in Macartney's observation was that courtyard life served to keep them mainly occupied, safe behind their four walls, but still with ample room to work and socialise.

Their names retain glimpses of a lost Beijing, including more than 600 named for nearby temples, 200 containing the word *ying*, for camps in what were once open fields, 132 with *qiao* in recognition of a nearby bridge, and some 62 named *cang* or *ku* for the presence of a nearby grain silo or storehouse.

Originally, many of these cloister-like dwellings were mansions for the well-off. The hutongs in the 'Chinese' city were simpler dwellings. But the 'Manchu' city amounted to a human shield around the Forbidden City, with the entire area subdivided into eight districts, one for each of the Manchu legions – four plain colours, and four bonus legions with fringed banners. The Wangfujing area, for example, was once home to the families of the Bordered White Banner. The Yonghegong area, around the Lama Temple to the north, was the octant of the Bordered Yellow Banner; the Drum and Bell Towers marked the border between that and the district of the Plain Yellow Banner.

In the days after the Manchu conquest, these were privileged locations. As the Qing dynasty stagnated, many devolved into slums, particularly in the period post-1911, when the bannermen of the Manchu city lost their imperial stipend. As time passed, particularly in the impecunious later Qing, or the egalitarian Communist era, many of the old *siheyuan* were subdivided, so that four or more families would have rooms in the same building. As modernity slowly took hold, the shared wells for clusters of hutongs transformed into standpipes, and ultimately into communal toilets/washrooms.

## Foreign Mud

Macartney was not wrong about the dust. Beijing was frozen solid in winter, baked dry in summer, and subject to horrific dust storms at other times. As described by Ellen LaMotte:

> These dust-storms are the curse of Peking, and of north China... It blows in straight from the Gobi desert and makes the late winter and the spring, particularly the spring, almost intolerable. Since our return we have been having dust-storms on an average of twice a week, big ones and little ones, lasting from a few hours to several days. There are two kinds: surface storms, when a tremendous wind blows dense clouds of fine sharp dust along the streets... and overhead storms, which... are a curious phenomenon: fine, red, powdery dust is whirled up into the higher levels of the atmosphere blown overhead by the upper air currents, from which it drifts down, covering everything in sight. On such occasions, there is frequently no wind at all on the streets, but the air is so filled with dust that the sun appears as in a fog, a red disk showing dimly through the thick, dense atmosphere.

Like the Mongols, the Manchu emperors did not enjoy Beijing dust, and preferred to live some 15km outside the Forbidden City, in a series of mansions and sculpted gardens near the Jade Spring, known collectively outside China as the Summer Palace.

The title is a misnomer. Although officially intended as a residence for the hot months, the Summer Palace proved irresistible for much of the rest of the year – its name falsely implying that the sovereigns were hard at work in the capital for longer than they actually were. They often packed up and headed for the Summer Palace as early as the Chinese New Year in February. At the actual height of summer itself, they were often nowhere near the Summer Palace, but sought even cooler climes many leagues to the north.

Kangxi, the Emperor of Hearty Prosperity, spent as much time at the 'Summer' Palace as his court responsibilities would allow. His son and successor Yongzheng, the Emperor of Harmonious Justice, effectively moved his administration to the gardens, and built extra palaces in its southern quarter so he could run the state without leaving them. By the time of Yongzheng's successor, Qianlong, the Emperor of Strong Prosperity, the Summer Palace was arguably more important to the imperial family than the Forbidden City itself.

The Summer Palace's finest garden was later known as the Yuanming Yuan (Garden of Perfect Brightness), the 'Versailles of the Orient', with a large lake, around which were clustered nine connected islets, each representing one of the ducal domains of ancient times. Its beauty was legendary, although not everybody was impressed; George Macartney, on the British mission of 1793, found it to contain a 'singularity of Chinese taste which... in truth is by no means worthy of our copying'. To Macartney's mind, 'the impropriety is glaring and argues sickly and declining taste, meant solely to display vanity and expense'.

But for almost everybody else it was a triumph of what is now called hybridity, as the Chinese emperors fell in love with the exotic imagery and trinkets of the distant west, with which they were plied by their Jesuit confidantes. Meanwhile, in the West, Europe fell in love with *chinoiserie*, as Jesuit accounts of the pomp and grandeur of China created a fad for porcelain, follies and oriental decoration. With bitter historical irony, the west would advance on the east for the next century, and the Summer Palace would pay the price.

Other landscaped gardens clustered nearby, including the Yihe Yuan (Garden of Nurtured Harmony), set around a former reservoir for old Beijing's water supply, now remodelled as a whimsical recreation of idyllic southern living, as Kunming Lake. Fairy-tale pagodas, statues, and pavilions were dotted around the lake and in the hills above, creating a false-perspective impression of being deep in the countryside, far away from the bustle of the capital.

A bronze ox, its back carved with a sacred spell to suppress flood-waters, gazes out over the lake, close to the majestic Seventeen Arch Bridge that reaches out to an island in the centre of the lake. The ox's presence suggests climatic troubles elsewhere – floods had heavily damaged the Marco Polo Bridge downriver in 1698, and its modern-day collection of stone lions mixes thousand-year-old originals with more recent carvings in the old style. The Emperor of Hearty Prosperity also renamed the river itself, changing it from the Capricious (*Wuding*) to the Eternally Pacified (*Yongding*), and hoping thereby to make it behave.

Floods, droughts and occasional famines were nothing new. But China was entirely unprepared for the arrival of the European powers. Towards the end of the Ming dynasty, European visitors were treated with amusement and condescension in Beijing. By the 1700s, the European community in Beijing was growing. The Russians were the first sizeable group, as emissaries of the great European power were able to literally walk all the way east to Siberia, and then south.

As marine technology advanced in great leaps, sea-faring nations were soon following behind, particularly the British. Then, as now, China was recognised as a market with gargantuan potential, ready to be moulded, coerced, or even bullied into cooperation.

Lord Macartney's kindly entreaties to the Chinese hid a greater urgency – the balance of trade between the English, who had a thirst for Chinese tea, and the Chinese, who famously claimed that they wanted for nothing. The American Revolution had cut off old trade routes across the Atlantic, and Napoleon was on the rise in Europe. The British took extreme measures by finding a new cargo that they could sell to the Chinese in exchange for tea – opium.

British popular myth, particularly in the old Chinatown of London's Limehouse district, would later suggest that the Chinese were a race of addled dope fiends. Such stories tended to avoid the inner truth, that they were made so by British salesmen. Opium ('foreign mud' to the Chinese) was grown and harvested in India, then shipped to south China, where the British became the drug pushers for an entire nation.

The exponential rise in the number of opium addicts in the south was a cause of concern to the Chinese. The government in Beijing tried to ban the sale of opium, and imposed severe punishments on its smugglers and sellers. But such well-intentioned decrees were of little use in the south, where forceful British officials such as Charles (Lord) Napier were demanding ever greater trade privileges. The Chinese administrator Lin Zexu wrote a stern letter to Queen Victoria, demanding that she rein in her pushers, but the message never reached the British monarch, who was herself an occasional dabbler in opium. The frustrated Lin eventually seized and burned all the opium in Canton in a heady conflagration in 1839 – the deed is celebrated as one of the tableaux on the Monument to the People's Heroes (see Gazetteer: The Centre). His bold act was answered with the arrival of a British fleet, brandishing modern cannons that far exceeded anything that the Chinese had to offer. In one of several actions later known as the Opium War, a fleet sailed up the Yangtze and effectively cut the Chinese empire in two, blocking Beijing's tax and trade conduits to the south. China was obliged to concede to the Treaty of Nanjing in 1843, an infamous document that opened certain Chinese ports to British trade, and permitted Christian missionaries into the country.

Chinese schoolbooks still regard this as the beginning of the 'Century of Humiliation', leading to a series of further incursions and unequal treaties, not halted until the proclamation of the People's Republic in 1949. Emissaries arrived from other countries, each determined to grab concessions on the Chinese coast ready to trade in the hinterland. Without a strong military or any means of resisting forces bolstered by the Industrial Revolution which had, until that point, largely passed China by, the Manchus were forced to concede several strategic towns and ports to foreign leases. The most famous, kept in foreign hands until the very end of the 20th century, were Hong Kong (UK) and Macao (Portugal), although China is littered with the evidence of other, forgotten concessions. Shanghai, Canton and Tianjin still have handsome boulevards built for Europeans, while Harbin's architecture still alludes to its former status as the 'Moscow of the East', and Qingdao retains a German brewery (Tsing Tao) set up by its European expats (see Food and Drink).

Equally embarrassing was the imposition of 'extraterritoriality' – the new arrivals treated the Chinese in much the same way as they had already treated the natives of America and Africa. It was decreed that Chinese laws and restrictions did not apply to Europeans – a stinging insult to the world's oldest continuous culture, which was now not even permitted to legally arrest, try or detain foreign criminals on its own territory. The cherry on the cake was the concept of Most Favoured Nation status, wherein any concessions granted to one power would have to also be granted to another. The imperial household in Beijing was no longer the master of its own country, and it was only a matter of time before this led to open unrest. Simple protests over food shortages or local injustice were often magnified along unwelcome political lines – in particular, much of the unrest in mid- to late-19th-century China dragged up the old spectre of the Ming dynasty, serving to remind the Han Chinese that even though they were suffering indignities at the hands of foreigners, their own rulers were themselves a clan from what was then regarded as outside China proper. As Manchu power weakened, whispers began that they had lost the support of heaven, becoming all the louder after 1853, when the Yellow River dramatically and disastrously shifted its course so that it flowed to the south, not north, of the Shandong peninsula, devastating thousands of square kilometres of farmland.

Religious and criminal movements suggested that it was time for a change. Ethnic minorities in isolated areas proclaimed rebellious enclaves that often went unpunished for years, while criminal elements took advantage of bad feeling towards the Manchus to paint their unlawful activities with a brush of Ming restorationism, or even the establishment of a completely new order.

In the south, the first sign was the cataclysmic Taiping Rebellion – more than a decade of violence that some insist on calling the Taiping War in recognition of the awful damage it did to China, and which led to more deaths than the First World War. Promulgating a bizarre mixture of revolutionary fervour and Christian dogma, the Taipings' leader was precisely the sort of enemy that China's indignity had created. Having failed the civil service entrance exams on several occasions, he woke up one morning and proclaimed that he was the son of God, waving pamphlets that he had picked up from a Christian missionary. His revolutionary movement, attracting the poor and dispossessed to his banner, would later be regarded as a forerunner of Communism, although none of its supposed higher aims were achieved before the Taiping rebels were wiped out, with cataclysmic loss of life.

Much to the embarrassment of the Chinese, the British took over parts of local government during the crisis. Even though Shanghai was in the grip of the Taipings, British customs officials continued to run trade in the area, collecting taxes on behalf of the impotent Chinese government. It was incidents such as this that would later be used to twist the arm of the government in Beijing, stripping it day by day of its powers and responsibilities, until the maritime customs of China was entirely ceded to foreign authority.

With the Russians pushing from the north, the Taipings uncontrollable in the south, and other foreign powers boasting that they could bring China to heel when the imperial household could not, the violence came to Beijing itself. When it did arrive, it did so in the form of European aggression, as the demand for more trade and diplomacy was delivered out of the barrel of a gun. In August 1860, a force of some 200 ships and 17,000 Europeans landed at Tianjin. They sent a delegation ahead to Beijing in the hope of negotiating a truce, but the Manchu general Sengge Rinchen ordered the emissaries to be tortured to death.

In October 1860, the combined French and British forces marched on the Summer Palace, expecting that the Xianfeng Emperor would be there. He and his entourage had already fled north to Jehol, leaving the new arrivals to wander, quite stunned, through the priceless artefacts of the gardens and palaces. Determined to punish the Chinese ruling class, rather than their people, for Sengge's atrocities, the British leader Lord Elgin ordered for the destruction of the Summer Palace. The Europeans took everything they could carry, smashing and burning whatever was left behind. Captain Charles Gordon, a young engineer with the British forces, reported that 'after pillaging it, [we] burned the whole place, destroying in a Vandal like manner, most valuable property... It was wretchedly demoralizing work for an army. Everybody was wild for plunder.'

Two days later, Lord Elgin ordered for the gutted buildings to be burned. A witness, Reverend R.J.L. McGhee wrote:

> Out burst a hundred flames, the smoke obscures the sun, and temples, palaces, buildings and all, hallowed by age, if age can be hallow, and by beauty, if it can make sacred, are swept to destruction. A pang of sorrow seizes upon you... No eye will ever gaze on those buildings... records of by-gone skill and taste, of which the world contains not the like. You have seen them once and for ever... man cannot reproduce them.

Antiques and plunder from the Summer Palace flowed onto the European market, with bargain hunters snatching up little bits of *chinoiserie*, even as they tutted at the behaviour of the French and English. The event remains a cause célèbre in Chinese history, a recurring topic in documentaries and fiction, as an example of the terrible damage wrought upon sovereign China by colonialists. Its most impressive recent manifestation is Liu Yang's book *Who Collects the Yuan Ming Yuan?* (Jincheng Press, 2013), a slablike coffee-table tome that attempts to reassemble the lost palace, tile by tile, by tracking down its pilfered remnants in museums, hotel lobbies and private collections all around the world. When the bronze heads of several zodiacal sculptures came on the global antique market in the 21st century, wealthy Chinese businessmen bought them back for the nation.

What is often not mentioned is how much the ruinous state of the Summer Palace owes to the Chinese themselves. The great dissenter here is Hope Danby, whose *The Garden of Perfect Brightness: The History of the Yuan Ming Yuan and the Emperors Who Lived There* (Regnery, 1950) is full of correctives, including the claim that the fabled zodiac animals were actually removed 20 years before the attack, at the order of an empress who hated them. This, however, still does not explain how some of them turned up in a Beverly Hills swimming pool a century later – at the time Danby was writing, she assumed they had been melted down.

It was the Manchu imperial family that decided to leave the Old Summer Palace derelict, and the Chinese common people who spent the next century sneaking over the walls to plunder it for any remaining statues, tiles and even bricks to re-use in house-building. According to Jasper Becker in *City of Heavenly Tranquillity*, this continued assault on the gardens went on as late as 1969, when citizens were raiding the Summer Palace for bricks to use in bomb shelters. The Summer Palace remained a location for squatters' housing and fly-tipping for the rest of the 20th century – its modern role as an icon of wronged China is very recent indeed.

The burning of the Summer Palace was yet one more sign of the end of the empire. The Xianfeng Emperor, nominal ruler of China, died aged just 30, leaving a child as his successor. Meanwhile, the new emperor's regents reluctantly agreed to the ultimate insult – the presence of foreign legation buildings in Beijing itself, in a 'Legation Quarter' just to the south of the Forbidden City. Beijing, and China itself, came to be regarded by the foreign powers in much the way that they regarded its six-year-old Tongzhi Emperor, as an ineffectual child that needed to have its responsibilities shouldered by others until it was able to fend for itself.

## The Origin of 'Peking'

The word 'Peking', which means nothing to the Chinese, carries within it at least part of the story of the foreign guests. When Lord Macartney came to China in 1793, he recorded the name of China's capital in his journal as 'Pekin'. Thomas Wade, a former ambassador who ended his days as Cambridge's first professor of Chinese, published the first English-language textbook of Chinese in 1867. Wade developed a system for romanising Chinese sounds during his long career in the diplomatic service, encompassing large amounts of time far to the south in Hong Kong, where the local dialect was much harsher and more guttural. The word *Beijing* was hence written in Wade's syllabary as *Peking*. He expected the P to be pronounced as a B, and the K to be pronounced as J. To actually make the sound 'Peking' with Wade's syllabary, a linguist would need to add the apostrophe-like voice markers and write it *p'e k'ing*.

Needless to say, this spelling, particularly as codified later on by Herbert Giles to form the Wade-Giles orthography, has eternally confused the non-specialist as to Chinese pronunciations. Matters were not helped by variation in pronunciation within China itself. Down in the south, where so many British visitors were concentrated in Hong Kong, the local language pronounced Beijing as something more like Bakging, which actually made the Wade-Giles rendering make more sense than it ought to. The confusion would continue for half the twentieth century, until Communist China, determined to free itself from the shackles of imperialist influences, even in the writing of its own language, approved the creation of its own romanisation system in 1958. The new system, which writes Beijing as 'Beijing', was not officially introduced until 1979, hence explaining the common discrepancy between generations. I grew up hearing the word Beijing, reinforced when I began studying Chinese under teachers from Mainland China. My parents' generation grew up hearing 'Peking', and many of them have yet to shake it off.

## The Empress Dowager

Regardless of the activities of the foreigners, it is often said that China's worst enemy in the latter half of the 19th century was a young widow of the Xianfeng Emperor, who would serve in various capacities as a regent for her son and then her nephew. Her most common name today is Cixi (1835–1908), but she is often known by the title that she initially received as the mother of Xianfeng's successor – the Empress Dowager. There is no statue of her; despite her immense celebrity and world fame in her lifetime, the Chinese are understandably reluctant to commemorate her.

Only 26 years old at the time of her husband's death, the Empress Dowager would dominate Chinese politics for the next 40 years. Then as now, it is the Empress Dowager, a cosseted concubine turned *grande dame*, who is most often held responsible for the spectacular demise of imperial China. This is, perhaps, unfair. Chinese folklore speaks of an ancient curse that predicted a woman of her clan would destroy the empire, but it seems overly simplistic to blame a 26-year-old woman for China's failure to hold off foreign predators and domestic revolution. In the early years of her reign, the Empress Dowager had more pressing matters at hand – forced to share the power of the regency with noblemen administrators and the late emperor's chief wife. Cixi was only a concubine, and received a position in the hierarchy solely for being the mother of the new emperor. Cixi may have been pig-headed, but she was a creation of centuries of stultifying tradition. She was barely literate – an extant edict in her own handwriting botches many characters – and wholly ignorant of the challenges that China would face if it were to square up to foreign pressure.

In 1872, her son came of age, supposedly bringing an end to the regency. But the reign of this Tongzhi Emperor lasted a mere three years, as he embarked on a series of ill-advised schemes, including an expensive attempt to repair the Summer Palace, and the demotion of many administrators who had annoyed him during the regency. Dead by 1875, allegedly of syphilis picked up in the brothels of Dazhalan, the Tongzhi Emperor left no heir of his own, prompting Cixi to adopt her three-year-old nephew, proclaim a new regency, and thereby buy herself another generation in power.

Cixi infamously used money earmarked for the modernisation of the Imperial Navy to renovate her holiday homes at the Summer Palace – hence the distinction in modern maps between the 'Old' palace, which is still in ruins, and the 'New'.

The shoreline of Kunming Lake still has the most notorious of the results – a marble terrace in the shape of a stylised paddle steamer, constructed at the Empress Dowager's order to give her another idyllic spot for moonlit banquets. It is an intricate, beautiful folly in every sense of the word, and an enduring monument to Cixi's blinkered grasp of reality, a fortune squandered on a playful garden ornament at a time when China's military struggled to hold off iron-clad foreign warships with antique wooden galleons.

It is easy to laugh at Cixi's frivolity, but some might argue that the renovation of the Summer Palace was not a bitch-queen's bid for luxury at all, but a desperate attempt by some of her officials to get her out of the way. For decades, factions in the Forbidden City sought to lure Cixi out of power with the one tool available to them – the good life. In one famous incident, palace officials waited until Cixi had expressly ordered that she not be disturbed during an opera performance, before taking advantage of the strict prohibition to pass and carry out an order of execution against one of her cronies. Similarly, we might suppose that administrators hoped to lure her out of Beijing so that others might be able to get on with the business of running the country – the Summer Palace is a mere stop on today's subway Line 4, but a hundred years ago was half a day's ride outside the city. Whether these men would have done a better job of holding off disaster, we will never know; their ruses never quite worked, and Cixi remained in charge.

No new ships were bought for the Chinese navy after 1888, leading to a humiliating defeat in the Sino-Japanese War of 1894–5, when Japanese incursion into Korea was met with brave but futile Chinese military intervention. Even as the Manchus clung to past glories, hiring officials on the basis of their family connections or mastery of classical texts, modern achievements in engineering and technology were changing the world. Beneath the notice of the Manchus, the history of north China was fast becoming tied to the fortunes of the railway that the Russians had built across Eurasia. With the establishment of Vladivostok on the Pacific, a name that ominously translates as 'Domination of the East', the Russian Empire could now move men and *materiel* swiftly to and from the Pacific. The Chinese had little say in the movement of Russian trains both around and through the Manchurian homeland of the imperial family; instead, the nearby island of Japan offered the strongest resistance. Seeing themselves as the 'British of Asia', the Japanese desired to be regarded as equals of the Western imperialists – which, for them, meant swiftly modernising and then demanding similar concessions in China to those received by the Europeans.

Meanwhile, the Foreign Legations took over an entire city sector, perilously close to the Forbidden City. Today, the city blocks behind and to the east of the National Museum, stretching all the way from Tiananmen to Wangfujing, often reward the wanderer with sights of forgotten consulate gates and foreigner-built banks, long since repurposed as Party branches and offices (see Gazetteer: Dongcheng).

Foreign ideas came with the invaders – a railway from Tianjin edged into the city by 1896, scandalously requiring the knocking down of a patch of wall, and a pitiful few Chinese and Manchu court officials attempted some reforms to strengthen China. They did so in the name of her charge, the Guangxu Emperor, leading the Empress Dowager to effectively dismiss him – although still nominally the Son of Heaven, he was kept sequestered in a palace while his supporters were rounded up and executed.

Beyond the walls of the Forbidden City, there was a rift across China between the small ruling class of Manchus, and the great masses of ethnic Chinese. Running low on friends, some among the Manchus fatally offered tacit support to one of the few uprisings that aimed to oust 'foreigners' without including the Manchus in their number. After further signs of Heaven's displeasure – flooding in 1898, then droughts in 1899 and 1900 – a society calling itself the Righteous and Harmonious Fist (*Yihe Quan*) rose up, supposedly to defend Chinese tradition from unwelcome foreign influences. Made famous by innumerable movies in the ensuing century, these 'Boxers' preached a form of martial art that purported to make its adherents invulnerable to bullets. Although this was soon proved to be untrue, the Boxer movement grew in stature, until armies of anti-foreign militia roamed China in search of missionaries and merchants to murder.

They reached Beijing in June 1900, at first in small groups, easily marked out by their red headbands and belts. What with the dust and the heat, observed the British journalist Putnam Weale, June was 'the historic month which has seen more crises than any other'. By 8 June, the embassy district was worried enough at rising reports of attacks on foreigners in Beijing to request permission for more soldiers to be brought up from Tianjin for their own protection. On 11 June, the Boxers struck close to home, murdering a Japanese diplomat, ahead of a mass Boxer invasion two days later.

The first Boxer assault on the Legations was repelled with a few gunshots. The following week, one of the Empress Dowager's wilier officials leaked a forged document that claimed that the foreigners had demanded the right to take over all administration in China. The angry Boxers were back in their thousands, trapping the foreigners and their families in the Legation Quarter in an armed siege that lasted for several weeks.

The siege of the Foreign Legations achieved worldwide infamy, uniting newspapers in Europe, America and Japan in their horror of the way foreigners were treated in China. It was an offence to the tender sensibilities of the Christian world, which regarded the activities of missionaries in China as sacrosanct, and the foreign media was soon rife with stories of brave soldiers fighting off sword-waving Boxer rebels, and devout missionary matrons cowering before rapacious rebels.

In a footnote to the violence, the writer Putnam Weale recorded an attempt by the besieged legations to dig under their own buildings to fight off Chinese sappers. Ten feet below the surface, the European diggers found scores of cannonballs, which they had presumed to have fallen upon what was once open fields in the days of the Mongol invasion.

> In other places, splendid drains have been bared – drains four
> feet high and three broad, which run everywhere. Once, when
> Marco Polo was young, Peking must have been a fit and proper
> place, and the magnificent streets magnificently clean. Now...!

It was not until the 14th August that a relief force arrived in the city, with Russians, British and Japanese racing for the chance to be the first on the scene. In fact, it was a Sikh soldier with the British army who was the first into the besieged area, crawling through a filthy sewer gate and along a ditch to announce the arrival of rescuers to the surviving residents. Chinese residents of Beijing had fled in their thousands, fearing the foreigners even more than the marauding Boxers. Cixi herself, disguised in peasant clothes, had been one of the anonymous figures in the retreating throng, abandoning the city from which her clan supposedly ruled the world.

While the relief of the Legations was a feel-good story all over the western world, the incident spelled disaster for Beijing and its surroundings. The city was partitioned between the rescuing forces, which imposed harsh military order on any Chinese who had not already fled the city. Beijing became divided under stern American-British-Japanese martial law for the following year, while the occupiers refused to negotiate with the Manchus until the Empress Dowager herself returned from hiding. Most Favoured Nation status even extended to plunder – German troops arrived late for the fighting, but still received a sector of the city.

The ensuing weeks saw Beijing torn apart by its new owners. Boxers had broken into the Summer Palace, under renovation after the Europeans' earlier looting, and raided the new buildings for timber. Back in town, entrepreneurs wrenched the famous astronomical instruments from the roof of the Old Observatory and sent them to Germany, where they stayed for more than a decade, until the Germans were obliged to give them back in the aftermath of the First World War.

The Empress Dowager did not return with her court until January 1902, arriving by train in what could have been a symbolic gesture of defeat. Instead, her arrival seems to have been regarded with elation by many of the Europeans present. When she offered them a little bow as she passed, they burst into applause. A similar selective amnesia about her involvement in anti-foreigner movements seemed to extend into the settlement over the incident, which left the Empress Dowager herself largely unaffected, although several of her officials were forced to take responsibility for the sequence of events, and paid with their lives.

But it was too late. The Manchus would never recover from the Boxer Rebellion. Russian incursions into the northwest, originally undertaken in the name of restoring order, were slow to retreat, leading eventually to the Russo-Japanese War of 1904–5 that saw Japan victorious and the Czar's authority fatally undermined. Reluctantly, the Manchus began preparations to modernise, sending a delegation to the West to learn its ways, although conservative opposition was still so strong that a suicide bomber attacked the delegates as they prepared to leave Beijing.

The Guangxu Emperor, still in seclusion, and the Empress Dowager both died in 1908, so close to each other that foul play was long suspected. The ailing Cixi ordered her eunuchs to carry her in a litter to Guangxu's chambers, where the two fading adversaries stared wordlessly at each other in a final, seething farewell. It was not until 2008, on the centenary of the emperor's death, that the *China*

*Daily* reported high concentrations of arsenic found in Guangxu's corpse.

Guangxu was succeeded by his nephew, another powerless infant, who screamed and wailed at his coronation, until his father tried to soothe him with the fateful words: 'Don't worry, this will soon be over.' The boy's reign title was announced as Xuantong, or Proclamation, perhaps implying a hope that China would soon be reformed by a series of imperial fiats. But he is better known today as 'Henry' Puyi, the Last Emperor.

# 6

# Northern Peace: 1912–1949

H IS PICTURE IS EVERYWHERE. His face stares thoughtfully
from every banknote from one *yuan* up. His statues and silhouettes clog every bric-a-brac shop and market stall. His giant
portrait graces the front of the Tiananmen Gate itself, gazing across
the square like a serene Buddha in a featureless grey jacket. Every
October, it is replaced with a fresh portrait that looks exactly the
same.

The man himself, or what's left of him, is on the south side of the
square, deep within the building that unkind critics have described
as resembling an unimaginative gymnasium. Although Mao Zedong
(1893–1976) had tried to get all Party grandees to agree to cremation,
he was overruled after his death, and laid to rest in this Mausoleum.
His body, carefully embalmed and pickled, spends each night in a
downstairs freezer, before being hydraulically raised back to its position in front of the troops of pious mourners.

Do not be daunted by the queue. Nobody can pause, so the long
line shuffles through with relative speed. The China visitor may even
feel a sense of elation, upon realising this is the only place in the entire
nation where one's passage will not be impeded by some buffoon
with a selfie-stick. After you have swiftly been ushered through to
pay your respects, you enter another chamber, decorated with the
massive characters of a famous poem, written by Mao in 1961 as a
'Reply to Comrade Guo Moruo'.

Mired in a complex discussion of whether or not a play about
one of the legendary Monkey King's battles contained allusions to
China's relationship with Soviet Russia, the poem appears to have
been reproduced here for Mao's apparent identification of himself

with the bold, impetuous Monkey King, cutting through the illusions that arise in a terrible storm, seeing the terrible white-boned demon that bears down upon him, and sweeping enemies from the sky like dust.

It is this version of Mao that is commemorated in his Mausoleum – the great helmsman who worked miracles, leading a revolution from a desert cave, and sweeping to power as the People's champion. Little is said about the Mao of the last 20 years of his life – the bitter, petulant mastermind of putsches and purges, the deluded visionary who led his people into cataclysmic experiments in social engineering that cost millions of lives.

## The 100-Day Empire

'Here we are in Peking at last,' wrote Ellen LaMotte, 'the beautiful, barbaric capital of China, the great, gorgeous capital of Asia. For Peking is the capital of Asia, or the whole Orient, the centre of the stormy politics of the Far East.'

Revolution had been brewing for decades, nurtured by overseas communities of Chinese, by secret societies that claimed to have been lying in wait since the fall of the Ming dynasty, and encouraged by democratic movements abroad. When revolution came to China, it came to the fractious south. Beijing, power centre for the old order, was slow to fall into step with the times.

Although still supposedly the Ruler of All Under Heaven, by 1912 the Last Emperor ruled only within his palace. Beijing itself was under the control of Yuan Shikai, an aging military man who had been called out of retirement in an attempt to keep order in the city. Yuan still had an army, and offered such an implacable resistance to the revolutionaries in the south that they were often obliged to play along with him. Although Sun Yatsen is remembered as the first president of republican China, he was in power only for a matter of days before he grudgingly resigned his post in favour of Yuan Shikai.

China hovered on the brink of fragmentation, as several provinces toyed with the notion of proclaiming their own independence. But while the notion of democracy and republicanism was strong in some places, in Beijing it seemed possible that the fall of the Manchus would merely lead to a new imperial dynasty. Yuan Shikai was declared president for a five-year term, soon extended to ten, and by 1915 he began preparations to become even more powerful.

It had been more than a decade since the last sacrificial rites were performed at the Altar of Heaven. Yuan Shikai eventually agreed to perform the rites himself, in a failed bid to establish himself as the new emperor. He proclaimed himself as Hongxian, the Emperor of Overwhelming Constitution, but his shambolic reign lasted for a mere 100 days.

Many histories paint Yuan Shikai as a corrupt official, but his defenders still insist that he was a loyal statesman frantically attempting to drag China into the 20th century by the most efficient constitutional means – if he demanded coronation, they say, then it was merely because the Chinese people did not understand the concept of political power that did not derive from a mandate of heaven. China had seen many dynasties come and go, and it would not have been the first time that a warlord had marched into Beijing, toppled the incumbent dynasty and then proclaimed his own. Republican, Nationalist rhetoric, with all its talk of democracy, may not have trickled down to the man in the street, particularly when the concept appeared so foreign.

It is only now, a century after the event, we know the Qing dynasty to have truly fallen. In 1912, many would have still expected, or hoped, or dreaded that some form of restoration might occur, either in full or in some sort of compromise that offered the Last Emperor a form of constitutional monarchy.

Yuan Shikai's government ordered that the Great Qing Gate, opposite Tiananmen, the Gate of Heavenly Peace, should be renamed the Great China Gate, removing the tablet on its eaves that associated the name of the edifice with that of the departed dynasty. But workmen were scrupulously careful as they removed its sign, deciding that it would be unwise to destroy the 'Great Qing' sign, since there was no way of telling at that moment whether the dynasty was truly over. Hedging their bets, they decided to wrap it carefully against knocks and scrapes, and to stow it out of harm's way in the gate's attic, ready for a swift, Orwellian reversal of nomenclature in the event of a sudden restoration. As they moved the sign to a suitably undisturbed corner, they found another tablet of similar size and shape, obscured beneath centuries of dust and grime. The writing on it read 'Great Ming' – it had been stashed in a similar fashion in the 17th century by their predecessors.

## The May 4th Movement

Impoverished China stood little chance of making a meaningful military contribution to the Great Powers fighting in the First World War. Japanese diplomats attempted to impose a series of invasive deals that would turn parts of China into a Japanese colony, leading China's own statesmen to fight back with a cunning ruse. China offered the Allies 'labourers in place of soldiers', sending some 140,000 workers to Europe to dig trenches, clear battlefields and work in factories, thereby freeing up able-bodied European men to fight against Germany. This ensured China a place at the negotiating table at the end of the war and, it was hoped, would prevent its Japanese 'ally' from taking advantage of the fall of Germany's colonies in China by occupying them itself.

The end of the First World War saw jubilant celebrations in Beijing. It was widely believed that the defeat of Germany would see the restoration of Shandong province to China, and with it, one might presume, the removal of any need for other foreign powers to keep up their bases on other parts of Chinese soil. The mood of the times, at least, suggested that the foreigners would now begin their retreat from China. However, many of the partygoers in the Beijing streets were unaware that Shandong had already been sold out, offered as security on a 20 million yen loan from Japan. When the subject of Shandong came up at the Paris Peace Conference, the Chinese were scandalised to hear that the German territory would be 'restored' not to China, but to the Japanese who had occupied it.

Protests broke out over both the loan itself and the perceived betrayal of Chinese interests; celebrants in front of the Tiananmen gate were replaced with student demonstrators. Whipped into a frenzy, they turned east towards the old Legation Quarter, where they planned on attacking the Japanese embassy. Armed guards presented too imposing a threat to the crowds, so they turned towards a new target. Instead of lynching the Japanese ambassador, they attacked the house of the Chinese Minister of Communications, whom they rightly suspected had been a prime broker in the Shandong scandal.

The fact that a paltry number of guards were able to frighten them away from the Japanese embassy speaks volumes. Although there were thousands of demonstrators, the number of active militants was considerably fewer – at first, only 32 arrests were made. Regardless, news of the incident spread throughout China and found support in many other cities. In Beijing itself, it was followed by strikes and a boycott of Japanese goods. Although the initial troublemakers had already been released, further demonstrations seemed much more wide-ranging – there were three thousand arrests, until the prisons of Beijing were overflowing. In June, Chinese diplomats refused to sign the Treaty of Versailles.

This uprising, on 4th May 1919, became enshrined in later annals as a crucial moment in the history of Chinese Communism. It was, so the Party historians later claimed, a moment when the Chinese people had had enough, and turned on the government toadies who had betrayed their trust. The fact that the protest happened in front of the Gate of Heavenly Peace, in the area we know better today as Tiananmen Square, was to make later Chinese governments incredibly jumpy at the sight of student protesters in the same place. The May 4th Incident was a landmark in the history of Beijing and the history of China, but for some it also set a dangerous precedent. Seventy years later, a government that regarded itself as the legitimate inheritor of the May 4th spirit would send tanks into Tiananmen Square to avert a similar event.

The May 4th uprising established student radicals as prime influences on decision-making, and brought the authority of the republican government into disrepute. It is no coincidence that a Communist youth group was founded in Beijing by 1920.

Meanwhile, Beijing lost its status as capital once more. The shaky republican state in the south proclaimed that Nanjing, the South Capital, was the new centre of the Chinese government. Beijing, perilously close to Russian and Japanese interests and the Manchurian heartland, had fallen out of fashion, and was renamed yet again, with a degree of blind faith, Beiping, or Northern Peace.

The years that followed saw the city buffeted by the interests of local warlords, resurgent republicans and Japanese intrigues. 'War and rumours arrived like clockwork,' wrote the novelist Lao She in *Rickshaw Boy*, 'every year during planting season.' Manchuria itself, homeland of the Qing dynasty, fell under Japanese control, and became a puppet regime ruled by the Last Emperor – he might have lost China, but he clung to Manchuria for a while longer.

Paul French, in his evocative *Midnight in Peking*, notes that 'between 1916 and 1928 alone, no fewer than seven warlord rulers came and went... they terrorised the city as they bled it dry'. The city was awash with soldiers and refugees – bandits turned militia, and victims of the distant Russian Revolution. Such straitened, lawless times brought dangers of their own to the city's heritage, offering irresistible temptations to the burglar and the pilferer, and threatening many traditional heritage items and locales. As noted Arlington and Lewisohn in their *In Search of Old Peking*:

> One might, perhaps, pass over minor acts of vandalism, such as converting historic palaces into modern restaurants and tea-houses; famous temples into barracks and police stations; cutting down ancient cypresses to sell for firewood; defacing age-old walls and tablets with political slogans, and so forth. But in many instances, historical buildings and monuments have actually been destroyed by official orders.

In 1937, trouble broke out over a seemingly minor incident at the Marco Polo Bridge, when Japanese officers demanded to be let into a fortified town nearby to search for a missing member of their company. When Chinese soldiers refused, the Japanese advanced across the bridge with tanks on 8 July. Chinese forces retook the bridge the day after and later agreed tentative terms with the Japanese, in which the soldiers agreed not to advance further. Despite this, Japanese tanks were in Beijing by 29 July – supposedly to defend the interests of Japanese businessmen and residents.

Northeast China had become a Japanese vassal, and the second 'Sino-Japanese' War had begun. Although it started as a conflict between Japanese occupiers and Nationalist Chinese defenders, in Beijing and other occupied zones, mainly along the coast, the war would escalate until 1941, when the Japanese attack on Pearl Harbor brought the Allied forces into the conflict on the side of the Chinese.

Beijing's antiquities suffered a predictable degree of neglect during the period. With no imperial family left to even consider maintaining the Summer Palace, the ruins fell even further into disrepair, raided for building materials by desperate locals, and even gaining a small cluster of shantytowns. Nor would the end of the war lead to reconstruction. The Japanese might have left, but the city was still in a dilapidated state, and suffered all the more when a new conflict broke out. The Chinese Communists and Chinese Nationalists, who had worked under a fragile treaty during the Japanese occupation, now turned on each other.

The Communists enjoyed strong support in the countryside, where local peasants often remembered comparatively few sightings of Nationalists during the campaigns against the Japanese. Before long, the civil war saw the Nationalists chased out of China, retreating to the offshore island of Taiwan, which retains a Nationalist (i.e. non-Communist) Chinese government to this day.

## The People's Republic of China

In October 1949, Chairman Mao stood at the balcony of the Tiananmen gate and proclaimed that 'The Chinese people, comprising one quarter of humanity, have now stood up.' He spoke to a crowd who had seen the worst of China's civil war. Tellingly, their various hurrahs still bore the taint of the imperial age, wishing Mao 'ten thousand years' as if he were a new emperor. Modern propaganda carefully rewrites the sense of it – the huge words on the gate today co-opt the idea for all, and not a single person. 'Ten thousand years to the great unity of the world's peoples,' they say, before the line is broken by a massive portrait of Mao. The line continues on the other side: 'Ten thousand years to the People's Republic of China.'

Never quite self-sufficient, Beijing had been cruelly tortured by the disruption of its food supply from the Nationalist south. Shortages had taken their toll in the closing days of the war, while money had been rendered meaningless by inflation at 8000 percent. The nominal restoration of its status as a capital had meant nothing under Japanese occupation. It did not become fashionable to call the city 'Beijing' again until 1949, and the city had been marginalised during a crucial two decades of technological development. A handful of main thoroughfares had been paved and smeared with rudimentary tarmac, but they had long since crumbled beneath years of neglect, the heavy rumble of military vehicles, and the inevitable consequences of Beijing's icy winters. The rest of the town was little changed from the days of the Boxers – more than two thirds of the residents still drew their water from wells, and few homes had electricity. The previous winter, people had been dying in the Beijing streets, with sweepers reporting 200 fatally frozen or starved in a single district. Those who made it to January 1949 were forced to endure a series of purges, as the victorious Communists hunted down thousands of Nationalist sympathisers and deserters in the city.

With old money only available in ludicrously high denominations, or bearing the unwelcome faces of pre-Revolution rulers, traders were forbidden to use anything but the new Communist notes. More pragmatic residents turned to barter or the black market, and money itself fell out of fashion. Some form of rationing, either of certain basic foodstuffs or certain cloth, remained in force for another 30 years.

The surviving palaces of the Manchu era were transformed into homes and offices for the Party faithful. Mao himself took up residence in the luxurious Zhongnanhai pleasure park to the west of the Forbidden City. But Mao and his associates had arrived in Beijing after years of deprivation as guerrillas in the wilderness. They had lived lives of relative austerity – even when able to put down roots in their Yan'an headquarters, they were essentially living in caves. Since many, including Mao himself, came from peasant backgrounds to begin with, they brought a new and radically uncomplicated attitude towards Beijing. Beijing in the early days of the Communist era still retained vestiges of its imperial grandeur; enough for Soviet advisers in the 1950s to develop a reputation as shopaholics and bargain hunters. But Mao would soon put a stop to that.

Much of China's imperial treasure had already been spirited away to safety by the fleeing Nationalists, at first stored in vaults by the government-in-exile at Chongqing. After the war, the treasures were relocated to Taiwan, where they remain today in one of the most richly appointed museums in the world. Their continued presence there remains a matter of Chinese diplomatic embarrassment, comparable to a similar argument of preservation and ownership to be heard between Britain and Greece over the Elgin Marbles. The chief difference is in the rhetoric – the governments in Taipei and Beijing both claim to be the rulers of China, and hence the most appropriate guardians of the antiquities. To this day, many priceless relics of Beijing's history are in the National Palace Museum in Taipei, the subject of recurring quarrels between the rival governments.

# 7

# Empty Spaces: 1949–1989

You won't find her in beijing. She was torn down and pulverised in swift order on a June day in 1989. But her sisters have sprung up in many places outside China. One of the most solid and enduring appeared at the heart of San Francisco Chinatown in 1994. There, in Portsmouth Square, a bronze statue still holds a flaming torch aloft. Any resemblance to the Statue of Liberty is purely coincidental; according to participants in the original construction, the students who created the Goddess of Democracy based her more on Soviet models than anything so provocatively pro-American.

The original was 33 feet tall, fabricated in a hurry from papier-mâché pieces over a metal armature. She had angular, almost Manchu features, and hair that seemed to be blowing in an imaginary storm. She was originally raised in an act and a place of defiance, raising her torch and scowling right across the road at the portrait of Mao on the front of the Tiananmen bastion.

There is very little evidence in Tiananmen Square that she was ever there. You can only sense her by her absence, by the large numbers of soldiers, police and conspicuous plainclothes security details on permanent vigil, and by the restrictions that turn simply crossing the road into an elaborate exercise in kettling and queuing. This, in a very post-modern sense, is a place where a statue once was, and it is only one of the most recent of Beijing's many, many monumental absences.

## Permanent Revolution

Mao's grand scheme for Beijing was like his plan for China itself, a state of permanent revolution, deliberately defying tradition. The most noticeable casualty was the city wall. At first, the damage was minor. Taking a leaf from the foreign railway builders of the 19th century, the town planners of Beijing smashed broad gaps in the old wall to allow better transport access. In the age of intercontinental ballistic missiles, there seemed little point in having such a small barrier to the outside world. Tradition itself was a dirty word – *tradition* meant centuries of imperial despotism, the suppression of the workers, the enslavement of women. Particularly strong in the early 1950s, when things were still friendly with Soviet Russia, was the desire to emulate Soviet modernism. This was most obvious of all in what was now called Tiananmen Square, created by clearing a space around the approach road to the Forbidden City, deliberately designed as a rival to Red Square in Moscow, and dominated by the giant column of the Monument to the People's Heroes.

Following Soviet Russia's example, China under Mao threw itself into vast, strenuous national initiatives, beginning with the First Five-Year Plan. Beijing, with its unreliable water and distant fuel supply, was unsuitable for large-scale industrialisation, but Mao was determined to turn it into a factory workers' city like Moscow. Many Beijing buildings were pulled down and replaced with brutalist state architecture, but nothing quite so brutal as the troubles that would follow among the Chinese themselves.

Merely because the Nationalist Chinese were gone, it did not follow that all was well. The Korean War plunged China back into a conflict on its doorstep, while the Nationalist regime in Taiwan continued to boast and brag that it would soon return to take China back from the Communists.

There was argument within the ranks of the Communists themselves – some supported the Soviet Russian model; others argued that there were unique conditions in China that required a uniquely Chinese solution. Further confusion broke out when it was revealed that the Russians themselves were in disagreement. In 1956, Nikita Khrushchev scandalised the Communist world by denouncing the late Josef Stalin, on whose personality cult Mao had modelled his own. It led Mao to invite denunciations of his own in his Hundred Flowers Campaign to encourage criticism of Communist progress, only to turn on his critics with the purges that followed.

The tenth anniversary of the People's Republic saw ten great architectural projects put in place, including the Great Hall of the People that dominates the western side of Tiananmen Square. But despite being the capital again and serving as a home to the Party leadership, Beijing lagged far behind many other towns in terms of its industrial production.

In an attempt to stave off the droughts and water shortages that had been a perennial feature of Beijing life from the time of the legendary dragons, the Communist leadership decided to build a new dam up near the tombs of the Ming emperors. Massive public 'voluntary' labour ensured that the dam was completed within six months, although it would appear that Communist engineers relied more on blind faith than they may have been prepared to admit. Once complete, the dam created a reservoir that is still rarely full – nobody had dared point out that many of the rivers flowing into it were dry for much of the year. Such gigantic but fruitless projects became a feature of the early Communist era – with much wasted effort, wasted time and wasted lives.

Another project, the Miyun Reservoir, had greater success, taming two rivers that were often prone to flooding, and creating a new water supply for Beijing. But even Miyun was not trouble-free – much of the early work was almost washed away during rainstorms in 1959, and early plans to use excess water to create a navigable canal were abandoned.

The Summer Palace began a slow process of restoration – Kunming Lake returning to its former function as a staging post for aqueducts into Beijing proper, while the surrounding area was reinvented as a public park. The ruins of the European assaults were left as they were, allowing Party faithful to reflect upon the implications of a weak China and foreign aggression.

The worst damage would come in the 1960s, when a China drunk on modernism decided to do away entirely with the walls of the Manchu city. They were pulled down to make space for a combined ring road and subway. Those pre-Communist buildings that survive in Beijing are lucky to have done so after years of warfare and a Soviet-inspired remodelling.

And then... a generation of children raised on the thoughts of Chairman Mao reached their rebellious teens and turned, in his name, on the Party itself. The Cultural Revolution, spearheaded by the fanatical Red Guards, sought to destroy much of what was left of old China. Many of those museums, temples and artefacts that had not been irreparably damaged in a century of unrest were destroyed in 1966. If it were not for the intercession of Premier Zhou Enlai, the Forbidden City and Beihai Park might also have been ruined.

Nobody would deny that putting hungry farmers and resentful teenagers in charge of national policy was bound to end in disaster, but there were other factors. Maoism's inventor was a man out of time, a peasant boy made good, undoubtedly bright, who studied hard to gain a Confucian education, only to discover that he had been born in an era where his classical knowledge was next to useless in an age of railways and power stations. He spent the rest of his life making up for it, refusing to admit that newfangled knowledge required more than willpower to master. His country origins and his classical reading often gave his pronouncements a sort of homespun quality to his audiences. To intellectuals, he could come across as pig-headed, ignorant or chillingly facetious. But to the masses, he sounded like a plain-spoken man of the people, always ready with words of managerial encouragement, always on hand with a few blindly optimistic parables of the utopia to come. When running a guerrilla campaign in the wilderness, it was enough to inspire his troops on to victory. It was, however, no way to run a country. Blithe dismissal of scientific reality was less of an issue when there were no engines to start or combine harvesters to service. But similar denials of bad harvests and poor production were to plunge China into a secret famine that killed millions in the early days of Communism.

Mao himself falls in and out of fashion. The current Party line regards him as a necessary evil and an important icon of unity– a leader that dragged China up by its bootstraps, only to come unstuck when the war was done and the time for peaceful progress arrived. On his deathbed, he offered dire warnings about the future of Communism, reminding his successors that they would have to stick to their guns for the next generation, lest the achievements of Communism be undermined by the temptations of the Capitalist free market. When those temptations won over, they were forced through by a faction within the Party that clung to Mao's maxim that leaders should 'seek the truth from facts'. The facts, they argued, had changed. If Mao were alive now, he would be reacting differently.

Far from creating enduring edifices and artefacts to benefit the people, Mao's era often created little more than empty spaces – gaps where buildings should have been, the absence of joy and freedom, shortages of food and other necessities, a lost generation of doctors and engineers, exiled to the countryside to 'learn' from the peasants, and thousands upon thousands of people quietly made to disappear.

## The Underground City

I thought it would be a journey like any other. I hailed a cab just outside the last remnant of the old city wall, by the newly restored watchtower. But when I asked the driver to take me to the Underground City, he suddenly lost the ability to understand me. I drew him the Chinese characters. He shook his head, and all but kicked me out of his cab.

The next driver was a similar case. Initially, he was so eager to snap up a rich foreign fare that he swerved across two lanes to get to me. But once I told him I wanted to go to the Underground City, he blinked blankly and said he had no idea what I was talking about. I pointed it out to him on the map, but he acted as if it wasn't there. Eventually, we reached a compromise; I named the corner of a street that was *near* the entrance to the Underground City. With some reluctance, fully aware that I would be heading off in search of a place he had sworn did not exist, he swung his car around and drove me there.

He dumped me without ceremony in a swish business district, and pulled away with a screech of tyres. I walked away from the wide road into a side alley, where the glass-sided buildings gave way to the patchy tiles and single-storey huts of a typical *hutong*. Melon-sellers pretended not to see me, and a tea vendor suddenly developed a great interest in his shoelaces. A mother grabbed two children close to her and scurried indoors, and I began to feel like the bad guy in a spaghetti western. Eventually, I found what I was looking for – a simple doorway in the street, flanked by a couple of small stone lions. I gingerly poked my head around the frame, and came face to face with a young woman in army fatigues, who all but spat her noodles out in surprise.

'Hello,' I said. 'Can I see the Underground City?'

She looked around herself in panic, and called downstairs for reinforcements.

'How did you find us?' she asked, setting down her noodles and standing almost to attention.

'There is,' I pointed out timidly, 'a sign outside in two languages.'

Two more women in camouflage arrived, and immediately began interrogating me. Their questions were polite queries delivered with an icy smile. Where exactly had I come from? How had I even heard of the Underground City? When I demonstrated that their secret base had half a page to itself in the Lonely Planet guidebook, they seemed faintly crestfallen.

The first stirrings of the Underground City were humble enough – bomb shelters sunk into basements all across the city at the height of Cold War fears of nuclear Armageddon. The emperors might be gone, but it only took the faintest whiff of paranoia in Chairman Mao for the whole city to be engaged with picks and shovels. Before long, news had drifted in from the Soviet Union of grander schemes – entire towns constructed inside mountains, designed to hold fast against atomic weapons.

Those first basement shelters were extended out and down by tens of thousands of conscripted workers, carved by hand. Two stories beneath the streets, human labour scraped spaces in the rock for a hospital, a cinema and a military arsenal. Although scraps of archive footage show the shelters cluttered and crowded, with residents growing mushrooms and raising chickens in apocalyptic squalor, today the tunnels are white and bare. An occasional portrait of Mao or Cultural Revolution slogan adds a scrap of local colour, and ante-chambers behind half-hearted partitions still seem full of junk like a Cold War jumble sale. My guide – a short, chirpy girl in camo-pattern clothes – accompanied me 'for my own safety', pointing out lesser tunnels devoid of electric light, and helping me across places where flooding forced us to balance on precarious duckboards. She was friendly enough, but something about her demeanour made me neglect to mention I learned my Mandarin in Taiwan.

There is a romance to the Underground City, in the bizarre way that it is presented to the outside world. Thousands of Beijing residents formed the work gangs that carved out the tunnels – George H. Bush, in his account of his own visit to the tunnels, claims that 70% of the digging was done by women. They dug in fear for their very lives, not just from foreign atomic weaponry, but also from their own leaders, who swore them to the utmost secrecy. This stealthy attitude persists – the Underground City was a well-known tourist attraction among foreigners, but kept menacingly quiet by Beijing locals, who are discouraged from visiting themselves. As for those like me who braved the obstacles, a theme park Cold War experience awaited – traditional Chinese inquisitiveness, which can often strike the Westerner as plain nosy, takes on an exotic, exciting sheen when doled out by girls dressed as soldiers.

But that is part of its charm. The Underground City was a creation of innuendo – unmentioned and denied, allowed to flourish in the imagination. Rumours clung to it like weeds. Wide-eyed visitors whispered that its tunnels extend for hundreds of miles beneath the city, that it forms an empty space beneath the ground like a negative Great Wall. Guides repeatedly claim that it stretches across 85 square kilometres, with at least one arm reaching out all the way to Beijing airport, and another to the port city of Tianjin.

Those few Chinese who are prepared to discuss it at all fall victim to their own country's media blackout. None are completely sure when it was built – it makes more sense for it to have been constructed in the 1950s or 1960s, but most seem convinced that it was dug in the 1970s. What little has been written about the Underground City highlights Russia's 'Brezhnev Doctrine', which threatened to invade any Communist country that did not adhere to a very Russian concept of Communism.

China and the Soviet Union had long been drifting apart, but disagreements over the nature of Communism were no longer matters for mere debate. Back in Moscow, Leonid Brezhnev made it clear that he was prepared to defend Moscow's brand of Communism by invading Communist states that dissented. Czechoslovakia and Hungary served as small but ominous examples. Beijing and Moscow risked turning into full-blown enemies. Chinese and Soviet troops clashed in 1969 over the border island of Zhenbao, and the septuagenarian Chairman Mao feared, with some justification, that open conflict might break out.

Except that is not quite true. The Zhenbao border skirmish was provoked by Mao himself, in one of several attempts to show the United States that he was no friend of the Soviet Union. At the time that many would have us believe that the tunnels were under construction, America was well and truly on a path to becoming China's friend. The only American invaders in Beijing were a startled team of ping-pong players, caught up in diplomatic intrigues when one innocently suggested it might be nice to see China, and was swiftly whisked away on a surprise tourist trip. When the coast was declared clear, it was Richard Nixon who made the greatest gesture of all, descending upon China for a historic meeting that helped lure China back into the international community. Surely, it was no time to be digging tunnels?

Were they even dug at all? The section on view to the public is impressive, but we only have the guides' word that it stretches across the entire city. They would say that, wouldn't they? Like the caves of Zhoukoudian, like the stones of the Great Wall, it is not the dank passageway itself that impresses, but the prospect of thousands more like it, lacing the Olympic city in Cold War stealth. But I have not seen a map of all the tunnels. Nobody has. Could it be that the Underground City is not a physical feature at all, but an ideological one – a frightening vision of a state that will stop at nothing to preserve itself? Not for nothing, the bulk of the visitors that come to the Underground City are overseas Chinese – excitable tourists from a Taiwan still viewed by Beijing as a rogue province, ready to hear outrageous war stories about the Communist war machine. They come to be amazed by the fanaticism of their one-time enemies. And then they buy a skirt.

Its largest room, a meeting hall ten metres below street level, was leased to a Jiangxi silk company. Just when one's day cannot get any more surreal, one is surprised by a lecture on silkworm cultivation and invited to take part in the picking and preparation of silk from cocoons. It is an enlightening lecture, and all the more strange for taking place in a secret bunker.

But what if the Underground City is real? How many Beijing banks have vaults that lie precariously close to a tunnel network? How many apartment blocks have foundations undermined by secret dwellings for forgotten Party cadres? One need merely look at the Great Wall to see what China is capable of. Why *not* dig a city beneath the earth? Perhaps there is another reason for the Underground City's stealthy status – the government prefers not to reveal just how big it is. Or perhaps much of it has already been repurposed. Just as Londoners in the Blitz used the Tube as a bomb shelter, perhaps Beijing refashioned much of its underground network for use by subway trains. It is, perhaps, not a coincidence, that whispered secrets about family members conscripted to dig an 'Underground City' appear to coincide precisely with the construction of China's first subway in 1969. It has long been suspected, but never quite confirmed, that the immense speed with which Beijing acquired a dozen new subway lines in the 21st century relied, at least in part, on the ability of town planners to repurpose miles upon miles of secret tunnels. There are, however, several remnants of it that have been acknowledged, including a basement shopping centre in Yuetan, the huge underground ice rink beneath Ditan Park, and, unsurprisingly, much of the tunnel system carved beneath the city by the Line 2 subway.

Opening in 1971, the Beijing subway was only one of many modern developments that heralded China's slow emergence from the hell of the Cultural Revolution. International flights returned in the early 1970s, along with telegraph and phone links to the outside world. A generation of angst at the United Nations was ended when the People's Republic of China took over the Chinese seat on the Security Council. The Nationalist Chinese on Taiwan were now diplomatic orphans, recognised by ever fewer other states, losing their friends one by one, and forced to come up with increasingly intricate ways of describing themselves as independent without saying the word. It was not until the early 1980s that China itself was prepared to declare the Cultural Revolution a mistake, and its instigators traitors.

Lord Macartney may have once expressed surprise at the close-quarter living arrangements of Old Beijing, but the Communist era saw residents packed even closer. Old Manchu mansions, outbuildings arranged around a central courtyard, were brutally repurposed to hold five, six, seven or more families. For much of the 20th century, Beijing's *hutong* neighbourhoods became synonymous with socialist squalor – the central wells of old replaced with single toilet facilities to serve all the surrounding buildings. Already forced into each other's laps by the small living quarters, Beijing residents were required to share what we might also optimistically call a 'bathroom' with over a dozen strangers.

Some, however, are more equal than others. The Party is still a major presence in Beijing. Turn north of Tiananmen Square, and walk the long straight road to the west of the Forbidden City, and the streets are hauntingly deserted. There are none of the traditional amenities – no roadside hawkers, photo shops, bistros or convenience stores. There are no beggars, no grannies selling postcards. Nobody is loitering, because anyone who does is moved swiftly along by the military police. This is where the political faithful live, as they did in Mao's day, clustered around the Zhongnanhai Park.

## The Goddess of Democracy

There is still discord (some might say debate) within the Party. This comes not from the handful of vestigial democratic parties, who simply rubber-stamp the decrees of the Communists. It comes from the people themselves. A state that owed so much of its origins to the May 4th movement could not easily end all public protests, particularly when Communism was supposedly founded on the will of the people. Late in 1978, the first stirrings of protest were felt again at what became known as the Democracy Wall – an innocuous section of sports stadium brickwork that became a magnet for posters and poems outlining things that needed to be done. Before long, the Democracy Wall was relocated to a nearby park by government order, and later protesters were obliged to have their comments screened by the authorities first.

Other protests showed unsettling signs of the rebellions of the past. The city erupted in violence in May 1985, when the home team lost a soccer match against Hong Kong, and thousands of hooligans poured out to vent their anger, somewhat ironically, against 'foreigners'. The unrest was met with a swift and tough crackdown on the offenders, and a hurried government apology:

> Last night's incident is the worst of its kind in the history of sports in the People's Republic, and the most damaging to China's international image. This type of ignorant and brutish behaviour is quite out of keeping with the stature of our capital city.

The year 1989 saw the most famous political protest in modern Beijing, a chilling reminder to the outside world. It began, supposedly, with the death of Hu Yaobang, a relatively liberal politician who had been forced to resign over contemporary student protests, and died soon after of natural causes. Some of his student supporters were soon in Tiananmen Square to show their support, and were joined by older members of the workforce, unhappy with recent price hikes. The Tiananmen Square protests thus already began in confusion, with disaffected Chinese assembling in the square and demanding... *something*, although it seems difficult to see what. *Democracy* seems to have been the buzzword – although the first stirrings of a free market was precisely what was causing the price hikes that had so angered some of the protesters in the first place.

Whatever this democracy was, it soon gained a new icon, courtesy of students at the Central Academy of Fine Arts, who assembled the famous Goddess of Democracy in just four days, a ten-metre statue of Styrofoam and papier-mâché, supported on a metal frame. Its size was carefully calculated for extreme visibility, since decades of propaganda had made the students amateur experts – if the army smashed down the statue, as they eventually did, it would be a powerful political statement in its own right. Until that moment, the Goddess was carefully placed in the square facing the giant image of Mao himself on the Gate of Heavenly Peace, defiantly brandishing a flaming torch.

By May 1989, there were hundreds of protesters camped out in Tiananmen Square, and all attempts to move them had failed. Sympathetic government officials had pleaded with them not to make a spectacle, with voices that became all the more strident as several hundred protesters resolved to go on hunger strike. Levels of government embarrassment climbed steadily as the date approached for a state visit by the Soviet leader Mikhail Gorbachev. Keen to avoid an encounter between a Russian reformer and student radicals, the Chinese government routed Gorbachev's motorcade through a series of outrageous detours to avoid Beijing's main thoroughfare.

With Gorbachev's departure, the gloves were off. At 10:30 pm on 3 June, the People's Liberation Army was sent in to clear the square. The use of the military to police a civilian disturbance ended in tragedy, an event remembered today as the Tiananmen Square Massacre. Protesters were forcibly removed from the square and from their enclave to the west of it – which would have placed them right outside the Party residences in Zhongnan Park.

Precise details, however, are hard to come by. Those who watched the whole thing on television were initially led to believe that thousands of people had died. These numbers seem based upon vague guesses supplied by harassed medical personnel and shocked foreign reporters at the scene, and may have confused casualties with fatalities. Not that a single death was justified, but in the years since the massacre, it has been difficult to find a list of the dead that climbs above two hundred. The trauma of the Tiananmen Massacre had far reaching effects. Liberals like Zhao Ziyang were drummed out of office, blamed for the very unrest that he had tried to dissuade. Martial law stayed in force until 1990, and might have been upheld for longer if it were not for Beijing's desire to normalise its appearance to the outside world. The economic reforms that some protesters demanded more of, and others wanted to stop for good, were briefly delayed in the aftermath, but soon reinstated in China's inexorable drive towards a freer market. In the years since the PLA smashed the fragile Goddess of Democracy into pieces, much stronger, more enduring replicas of the statue have sprung up in overseas Chinese communities – most notably on the western seaboard of North America, where they continue to stir controversy between supporters and opponents of the Communist regime.

In the hours leading up to the attack, there was a debate among the protesters as to how they should meet it. Many were keen to leave the square peacefully, although as on May 4th seventy years earlier, a militant element was determined to fight back. To hear the army's version of events, it was these militants, armed with petrol bombs, who fought back against the PLA. There were military casualties, too, in the Tiananmen Square massacre, eliciting considerably less sympathy from the international community.

One soldier was faced with an intense diplomatic situation when the path of his tank was blocked by a lone figure. The unidentified man clutching two carrier bags, who faced down an entire tank column, became Beijing's most famous resident. In an iconic moment of the 20th century, the unknown rebel harangued the driver of the lead tank about his mission, until passers-by wisely dragged him out of harm's way. His precise identity and his ultimate fate remain one of the mysteries of Beijing history.

Twelve years after tanks rolled across Tiananmen Square, the International Olympic Committee announced that Beijing would become the centre of the world once more. In August 2008, the city would play host to the Olympic Games.

# 8

# Beijing in the 21st Century

J IANGUOMEN, the 'Gate of Building the Nation', is long-gone, but still lends its name to the street that once went through it, and an intersection where it once stood. Its 'inner' and 'outer' stretches are divided by a giant broken-arched rainbow, its multiple colours illuminated at night. The local expats usually call it the 'Big Gay Rainbow', associating it with Gilbert Baker's globally-recognised 'Pride Flag' celebrating diversity in the gay community. That, however, has got nothing to do with it.

The Rainbow on Jianguomen and a twin arch on the far side of the city were intended to represent something very different – the 'return' of Hong Kong to Chinese sovereignty in 1997. The wording is deliberate; what was known as the 'handover' in Anglophone media, regarded by many with caution and melancholy, was a moment of great jubilation throughout much of the Chinese community, even in non-Communist Taiwan. For China and the Chinese, 1997 was a watershed in China's recovery from a century of humiliation, and an important point on the road to greatness. The 21st century, thought by many to be China's prospective new golden age, was only a few years away, and the Rainbow marks its advent. For the China-watcher, it is a little ironic, and perhaps fitting, that hardly anyone who passes the big, glowing, multi-coloured installation knows what it actually represents.

THE HANDOVER WAS only one of China's improvements on the road to modernisation and globalisation. The hosting of the Olympic Games was another. Its legacy can be seen in concrete form in the north of the city (see Gazetteer: Chaoyang), in the architecture of the Olympic village, and ongoing attempts by the authorities to find some way of using the facilities for posterity.

Beijing's involvement with the Olympics is surprisingly recent. China only participated in the games on four occasions before 1956, the period of the first Five Year Plan, and had been totally absent thereafter until 1984. The era of the Cultural Revolution killed more than just education and development; it even killed sport.

The achievement of actually hosting the games was an incredible learning curve – a superhuman effort, all the more daunting considering the low ebb of international opinion in the wake of the Tiananmen Massacre. Planning began in February 1999, when President Jiang Zemin addressed a national conference in Beijing on 'Promoting the World's Understanding of China.' The President's inaugural speech emphasised the need to 'teach the world' about China; amid suggestions that China might also have something to learn from the world, he urged his people to educate the rest of the world about China's own history.

Beijing hosted the Asian Games in 1990, pouring US$300 million into new building programmes for the expected guests. Some of the initiatives were more cosmetic – the plastering over of bullet holes at the edges of Tiananmen Square, and the repaving of avenues to remove the tell-tale tank tracks gouged in the road.

Even so, China would not be forgiven so easily. Representatives of the International Olympic Committee (IOC) arrived in 1993 to discuss Beijing's bid to host the Olympics in 2000, where they were regaled with snazzy documentaries about China's rich cultural heritage, and the bizarre promise by Beijing's mayor that all the delegates would be immortalised in a plaque on the Great Wall, if they only agreed. Ironically, part of the Chinese pitch for the games rested on totalitarian guarantees of an obedient population, assuring the IOC that there would be no protests or trouble. In a strange reversal of the drab Mao era, schoolchildren were instructed to dress in brightly coloured clothes, and bussed in to Tiananmen Square by the thousand. Meanwhile, behind the scenes, coal-burning heaters and smoky factories were shut down for the duration of the IOC's visit – in order to ensure clear blue skies over the city, many citizens were deprived of hot water and sent home from industrial jobs.

The Beijing 2000 bid was an impressive effort, all the more remarkable considering how swiftly the Chinese had to learn to play the international game. But Beijing's cosmopolitan status was still doubtful, with relatively few international flights, and a population lacking in competent English skills. The smog-busting ruse had also failed – the delegates thought that environmental protection in Beijing was still substandard. Crucially for a global sporting event that relied on the attention of the world, Beijing's telecommunications were deemed not up to global standards.

Yet none of these problems was a deal-breaker – there was still a chance that the Beijing bid might be successful, if the organisers were able to give the appropriate assurances. According to one rumour, the final straw, tipping the decision in favour of Sydney by just two votes, was an ill-advised moment of old-school Party bluster, when a Chinese official suggested that China would not bother with future Olympic games if it failed to win the 2000 bid. It was exactly the wrong thing to say to the IOC. The Olympics' own mission statement emphasised international understanding, global cooperation, and competition in friendly rivalry; it was not about to cave into retaliatory threats or pre-emptive sulking.

## The 50th Anniversary

The failure of the 2000 bid clearly hurt the Beijing committee, which had accomplished amazing things, even if ultimately unsuccessful. In the aftermath, Beijing temporarily retreated in on itself, announcing a Five-Year Plan of renewal and renovation, which improved conditions in the city for the 50th anniversary celebration of the founding of the People's Republic – an aim that would please the Party faithful without the loss of face that a second bid on the international stage might have occasioned.

Crucially, the city's government finally admitted in February 1998 that Beijing suffered from some of the worst air pollution in the world, with the ever-present dusty winds from the western deserts augmented by coal-based pollution and the usual smog of an industrial centre with a growing population of automobiles. New traffic laws denuded the streets of some of the worst smoke-belching vehicles, but also reduced the number of bicycle-only lanes in what had once been a city where pedals and the pedicab were the default form of transportation.

Beijing residents were encouraged to change not just their city, but also themselves, in a programme to teach them better manners – less spitting in the street, (punished, Singapore-style, by a US$6 fine), improved hygiene, and a better sense of personal space. The 11th of each month in the year preceding the Olympics became 'Queuing Day', in which locals could receive awards for displaying a more internationally acceptable grasp of the importance of standing in an orderly line and not cutting in. A nine-point pledge appeared on billboards all over the city, demanding that 'civilised residents' abide by maxims of acceptable behaviour. Some, such as an admonition to practise family planning, were old-school Chinese Communist slogans. Others, such as the commandment to 'love science and respect teachers' were powerful about-faces from Mao-era contempt for learning. Still more, such as a demand to 'be polite to guests', seemed aimed at preparing Beijing citizenry for an influx of thousands of Olympic visitors. A unit of 'English police' was formed – in fact two scholars, one Chinese and one English, tasked with hunting down bad spelling and grammar in Beijing signs, in order to avoid embarrassing howlers.

Beijing citizens were expected to learn English, with local workers encouraged to take lessons, and useful phrases cropping up in new sections of newspapers. In particular, Beijing taxi drivers were singled out as the likely front line of many foreign visitors' interactions with China, since it was widely understood that foreigners would leap upon the chance to be chauffeur-driven around town for an average cost of US$2 a trip. Beijing cab drivers must hand out numbered receipts, and most appear to have been well drilled in putting the customer first.

## The Demolition Derby

Jasper Becker, in *The City of Heavenly Tranquillity*, suggests that the death knell for old Beijing was sounded much earlier, in 1982, when the government made a drastic change to the law and constitution. Urban land was reassigned to the ownership of the state, matching similar transfers in the countryside, and turning every Chinese home-owner into a mere tenant. At any point, with only minimal warning, the authorities could snatch land back from its occupiers, and were only obliged to compensate them for the loss of the building materials on the site.

With residents discouraged from spending their own money on renovating a building that could be taken away from them at any moment, a decade of decay set in. A second punch landed in 1992, when authorities 'surprised' by tumbledown districts introduced new legislation that allowed for the 'reform of dangerous residential buildings'.

'In this way,' writes Becker, 'a local government could decide to level an entire neighbourhood whenever it saw fit, simply by declaring it a slum'. Throughout the 1990s and the 2000s, investors with the right connections were able to requisition whole city blocks – handy for Olympic facilities, and in the years since, for the sudden mushrooming of skyscrapers, shopping malls and other large-scale developments.

One of the most severe casualties of Beijing's remodelling was the old *hutong* lifestyle. A temporary measure that long since outgrew its usefulness, the conversion of 19th century homes into 20th century hovels was no longer desirable, not merely for matters of hygiene and living standards, but for simple economies of space. *Hutong* buildings rarely climbed above a single storey, whereas modern China favours huge tower blocks stacking residents on top of one another. Ousted residents were either relocated to satellite towns or offered an apartment in the tower that sat on the site of their former house. Few, however, could resist the temptation to cash in the increased value, selling their windfall residence before the paint was dry, and effectively exiling themselves from the city that was once their home.

More reforms were part of the 'Toilet Revolution', as Beijing locals were instructed in suitable behaviour. Decades of *hutong* life had left Beijing residents with little sense of privacy, and many foreign visitors returned with shocking horror stories of dirty holes in the ground, and communal shit-pits. China gained its own ideal toilet exhibition, designed to introduce the no-nonsense locals to the concept of closing a stall door, or indeed the existence of stall doors in the first place, and, in fact, stalls.

The government began hunting down Beijing's growing underclass of peasants and vagrants from other parts of China, lured by capitalist-inspired dreams of finding their fortune, and often left to subsist in off-the-grid shanty towns and overpopulated flophouses. In September 1999, just one month before the 50th anniversary of the People's Republic, officials initiated a purge of the 'Three Withouts': those without papers, those without residence permits, and those without legitimate and permanent income. Thousands of beggars and tramps were rounded up, while a separate modernisation programme, using the 1992 law as a hammer, demolished 2.6 million square metres of 'illegal structures' – lean-tos, huts and sheds used as accommodation by the rural poor. A common symbol on Beijing walls was the character *chai* – a hand holding an axe – marking any building for destruction, an empty space in waiting. In a moment of foolhardy architectural protest, some new buildings, constructed as part of the renewal protest, also gained a *chai* graffito, scrawled on their walls by unknown parties who disapproved of the speed and nature of change.

The area around the Forbidden City was beautified with a wrecking ball, with the demolition of hundreds of Qing dynasty mansions, now dilapidated by decades of communal occupation – today, of all the noble dwellings in the area, only Prince Gong's is still standing and open to the public (see Gazetteer: Xicheng). Further out of the centre, officials disbanded and discouraged street markets, leading to a brief but telling citywide shortage of fresh fruit and vegetables. There was also a minor controversy over the demolition of Xinjiang Alley – a street that had achieved a gourmet reputation with ex-pats and students for its *halal* Uyghur cuisine. Despite grumblings from foreigners in Beijing, Xinjiang Alley was wiped off the face of the earth in February 1999 – many of the establishments had been built on public land without permits, and hence stood little chance of resisting the demolition order.

Despite the controversies over the approach of the 50th anniversary celebrations, they also served to prove how foreign attention could lead to local reforms for the better. The upheavals were unwelcome, even when undertaken in the name of Communism and not the Olympics, but also led to government initiatives to sweeten the pill with 'good news' programmes. Seemingly in an attempt to counter-balance complaints, the people in the rest of China were told that social security pay-outs were to be increased, and civil servants would receive a 30% pay-rise, backdated for several months. But to many outside observers, the 1999 anniversary celebrations were another sham, with the obligatory military pageant, and counter-productive security measures that forced people who lived on the route of the parade to keep their windows shuttered throughout.

In February 2001, Beijing was prepared to try again to impress the IOC, with the arrival of an inspection team to see how the city had developed. To local residents, it was a repeat of the previous attempt, with a mass mobilisation of street-sweepers and painters before the

IOC's arrival, and a round-up of the usual suspects. This time, the plan worked, and the IOC announced on 13 July 2001 that the Olympics in 2008 would take place in Beijing.

A decade after the Games, their paraphernalia can still be found in junk shops and the more ramshackle shopping centres. The city had not one but five Olympic mascots, in what the Olympic adverts claimed to be a 'message of friendship and peace', but which really seem to be an acknowledgement of the only force more powerful than *realpolitik* – marketing. The cartoonish Olympic mascots were a menagerie of Chinese creatures, conceived as 'collectable' for all those capitalist visitors, whose children should pester them to bring back not one cuddly toy, or action figure, or key chain, but five. The mascots were a colour-coded team; traditionalists might hope to link them to the Chinese elements, but their conception owes more to branded Japanese team-shows like the *Mighty Morphin' Power Rangers*, their nominal leader a fiery personification of the Olympic flame. Foreign visitors were exhorted to collect the entire set as if they were Pokémon or some other consumerist craze, from the ubiquitous panda and the predictable fish (for water sports) to a politically sensitive Tibetan antelope. The fifth mascot character was a spirit of the air, appearing on logos for such pursuits as badminton and fencing. As a bird-totem, she was a Swallow, personification of the ancient Land of Swallows, and a symbol of Beijing's long-term poetic associations.

## Modern Ghosts

The Olympics were a programme of wide-scale renovation for Beijing, easily equivalent to the sweeping transformations of Khubilai Khan or the Yongle Emperor. Every nation that holds the Olympics ends up asking itself the same question. Are we really helping our own people? Will this really improve our infrastructure? Or will there be hungry beggars in ten years, huddling for shelter in the shell of an empty stadium? Beijing has seen many Five Year Plans and grand schemes; it has been razed to the ground on numerous occasions. Will this latest project bring true good, or will it create more discord than it quells, instilling the local poor with grand expectations, and a grand sense of entitlement to something that the future may not be able to provide?

It used to be that as the tourist reached the final approach to the Great Wall at Simatai, a crowd of hawkers waited hungrily. With little to do but loiter at the top of a mountain, they had engineered a pecking order based on the time they reach their pitch, and seemingly agreed to allow one tourist each. Each group of visitors hence acquired a symmetrical platoon of men and women clutching weather-beaten satchels, earnestly trying to sell the standard accoutrements – postcards, dog-eared guidebooks, and Republican-era silver dollars with authentic dirt. Beggars were not so much banished by the Olympics as rebranded. A beggar with a packet of postcards is officially a beggar no longer, although he can be just as persistent.

'We are farmer,' they would say in broken English, pointing at the fields far below. 'This: tower,' pointing at the nearest battlement. In the logic of Chinese etiquette, this made them guides and you their grateful employer. They did not take kindly to being told that you did not need their assistance, as by the time they found this out, they had already lost their place in the queue on the ridge, and had to wait for their next turn.

But the hawkers of Simatai have themselves disappeared into history, swept away and repurposed as the city expands out to meet the countryside. Simatai, once a dusty hamlet near a reservoir, has been reborn as a 'Water Town' – an *olde worlde* evocation of Qing-dynasty life, with yuppie apartments scattered around the edges of picturesque lakes and charming canals. Artisans labour in boutique workshops, all in the shadow of the Great Wall. It all seems like a deliberate echo of the similar tourist-traps that are dotted around the suburbs of distant Shanghai. Or, perhaps, to the more historically minded, it recalls the quaint living-theatre of traditional China that the Empress Dowager once arranged at the Summer Palace, where she could wander through an old-fashioned market, and tell herself that nothing would ever change. Now, the farmers of Simatai have a new performance, *pretending* to be traditional herders and weavers, putting on a show of sowing crops and gathering harvests to add a sense of traditional authenticity. They dress up as the people that they once were.

Although Beijing is now part of the 21st century world, it still has its ghosts – or more accurately, immigrant ghosts from other parts of China. Folktales and rumours no longer spread from tavern to tavern, co-opted into musical acts and storyteller routines. Instead they leap across the Internet and television. Beijing children terrify each other with tales of a haunted bus stop, where a disembodied voice calls out to the unwary, asking them the time. Damnation awaits anyone who is foolish enough to answer without turning around – it is the modern equivalent of the black-cloaked murderer of Beihai Park, but the story, like many modern Beijing residents, is not a native. Instead, it has entered local folklore from Hong Kong, where it first appeared.

Beijing is the Cinderella figure, left in the shadows, never previously invited to the capitalist ball. Hong Kong is the brassy, loud, ugly sister, the one that got all the attention and all the money, suddenly swanning back home after a century of foreign suitors, dripping with glitz and glamour and high-tech trinkets. In the 21st century, Beijing is reinventing itself as a class act – the place with all the history and the monuments, the place where the emperors lived, the place where the government is, and not forgetting the Eight Sights. But while Beijing might have the ruins of the Old Summer Palace, and the memory of its destruction, Hong Kong has a full-sized replica of the Summer Palace in its heyday – an ongoing argument of style versus substance.

With Tiananmen still an international embarrassment, the Chinese government embarked on a series of initiatives designed to present a different side of Beijing – just as the Emperor of Perpetual Happiness had tried to fake historical continuity with his Eight Great Sights, the People's Republic pushed for the reinvention of many Beijing landmarks. Paramount among these was the grounds of the New Summer Palace, its renovation speeded up, redefined as a site of historical pilgrimage. The ruins of the Old Summer Palace, however, were left in their tumbledown state.

Every now and then, an antique stolen in the sack of the Summer Palace comes on the international market. On the most recent occasion, China was forced to buy back what was rightfully its own, at a London auction house, at a cost of millions of dollars. A debate has raged for decades about the best manner to deal with the Old Summer Palace, with some officials arguing for the construction of a replica of its glory days, while others push for the original ruins as a far more evocative and moving sight. When one talks of tourists in Beijing, one is often talking of European tourists, and there is a strong and persuasive case for confronting such visitors with the ruins of their states' earlier military interventions.

**Interesting Times**

Real Communist-era treasures, such as the delicate propaganda posters that once hectored the faithful to Respect the Party and

Destroy the Capitalists, are much harder to come by – their very fragility helping their value on the foreign market. But Beijing in the Olympic age would really rather prefer that the foreign tourists stayed away from the socialist era. Sites and opportunities are certainly available to detail the achievements of Communism – particularly the Military Museum (see Gazetteer: Xicheng), occupying a forbidding Soviet-era power station, and detailing the various injustices visited upon China by foreign powers. But the Communist era itself, with its headlines of grain harvests and tractor designs, is something of an off-colour joke, amusing in a dreary way for a while, until the poverty, persecution and purges of the Cultural Revolution stifle the smiles.

Upon seeing that I genuinely do have an interest in Mao-era propaganda, an antiques seller shyly proffers a small stack of crumbling posters – carefully aged, if not actually old. Her face goes as red as the East when I happen upon a slogan calling for the downfall of America.

'Times back then,' she says, 'were *interesting*.'

The great halls and staircases of the Forbidden City; the soaring towers of the Great Wall and the statuesque beauty of the Ming Tombs are much more likely to attract tourist dollars, at least from capitalist tourists. Once an embarrassment to town planners, the *hutong* alleys of Beijing are just as much a part of the modern city's heritage as the Forbidden City – perhaps more so, since a visit to them often pays directly into local pockets, instead of government coffers. Pedicab drivers offer tourists trips around the few remaining *hutongs* in the city centre, where tourists can gawp at Qing-style buildings, and the sight of people living on the edge of rural poverty, so close to the luxurious apartments of the Party faithful. But these, too, are dwindling, turning into theme-park re-enactments of what once was a genuine way of life, and is now unaffordable to the people who work there. But this is not a uniquely Chinese experience – modernity exerts similar pressures on us all.

The Marco Polo Bridge is still where Marco Polo said it was, although much of what he said *about* it no longer holds true. It is not 'ten miles outside the city', since the metropolis of Beijing has sprawled across every scrap of available land in the place where once there was just an endless tract of marshland waving with reeds and thistles. Nor does the bridge serve its original purpose – not long after being given its new name by the Emperor of Hearty Prosperity, the 'Eternally Pacified' Yongding River took the hint and went away for good, leaving the bridge literally high and dry. Although floods and rains and the outflow from a 1950s reservoir may occasionally give it something to span, the bridge usually crosses little more than a shallow dip in the landscape, so overgrown that it looks more like parkland.

A few steps away from the ancient bridge, a sturdy concrete flyover takes care of modern traffic, although the bridge's 20th century companion is less welcoming to pedestrians. You can still walk across the Marco Polo Bridge, but now it costs you two dollars. There is still a trading post there, but it is a small and sorry open-air 'antiques' market selling bits of fake jade, Chairman Mao lighters, *feng shui* compasses and doubtful fossils. Always, *always* there are the Republican era silver dollars – big round coins like Jubilee Crowns, bearing the fat, bald head of Yuan Shikai and smearings of dirt for that extra touch of authenticity. There were over 184 million minted, and all appear to be still in circulation, all boldly proclaiming that they are worth one dollar, all retailing for twenty and up.

The Great Wall remains the most powerful of symbols – its image is the first that any China visitor sees, snaking across every tourist visa. Entrepreneurs are redeveloping many more sections now, attempting to revitalise the economy of the mountains north of Beijing by making a visit there about more than just seeing the Wall. Giant billboards out towards Simatai exhort tourists to come in the dead of winter, when they can ski in the Great Wall's shadow. The wall has also gained a modern, virtual analogue – the Great *Firewall* of China that blocks access from new forms of Western barbarity: our news, our erotica, our idle gossip. If you have Google as an Internet homepage and a browsing habit that swings over to the BBC website several times a day, it can be a surprise to discover that those sites are simply not available to the internet user in Beijing.

The concept of Heritage does finally hold some sway in Beijing. A Kentucky Fried Chicken franchise was ejected from Beihai Park after local pressure groups called it a capitalist step too far. Similar controversy surrounded the Starbucks in the Forbidden City, which gained a kitsch appeal among tourists before its unceremonious removal in July 2007 – the very silliness of it had a certain charm, akin to finding a Hello Kitty shop in Westminster Abbey. Despite my arch disapproval, I still feel compelled to use the ATM in the Forbidden City, just so I could say that I had. I took money from a hole in the wall at the Centre of the World, and was charged five dollars for the privilege.

There are mixed feelings all round about the incursion of Western-style consumerism into the Forbidden City. After all, don't we *want* them to be more like us? We want them to buy mobile phones, don't we? We want them to listen to the Beatles. We want them to sign trade agreements and consume along with the rest of us. As green politics rises to the fore, we also would like them not to make the same mistakes as us regarding pollution, demolition and emission, but perhaps it is already too late.

Tradition is a double-edged sword. Chinese tradition crippled women for a thousand years with foot binding; it castrated thousands of pauper boys to allow them to work in the palace; it tortured untold millions. The Forbidden City is no longer forbidden or forbidding – it welcomes visitors with their open wallets. Its brand identity, after all, is kept relatively muted, and it does good business – who are we to stop the Chinese from having a coffee at the Centre of the World, where eunuchs once tried to keep bicycles and eyeglasses away from the last emperors. The Western world already has its junk food and its corporate beverages, like it has the internal combustion engine and the nuclear power plant – should we begrudge the Chinese their coffees Venti and Grande, in the same way we begrudge them greenhouse gases?

But nor is modernisation a bed of roses. The rush of the modern is what hacked the Chinese coast up into treaty ports. Our desire to make the Chinese in our image is what force-fed them opium, and smashed railway lines through ancient city walls. There are poor in London, too, in Washington, in Paris. Beijing was there before them all.

# 9

# Eating and Drinking

THERE ARE MANY TRAVELLERS for whom food is nothing but fuel, best swiftly ingested before heading off to the next destination. This is not the way to approach China, where the best food in the world, everywhere from street stalls to banqueting halls, should most definitely be part of the experience for any visitor.

Restaurants come and go with great frequency, such that I am reluctant to point to many single establishments, apart from a couple of well-known names that appear to have wriggled onto fixed tourist itineraries. In the last year alone before I delivered this second edition to the publishers, Beijing lost two of its best Yunnan and Xinjiang restaurants, the quality at a major duck restaurant took a turn for the worse, and one of the city's friendliest teahouses suffered a hostile and damaging take-over by one of its investors. For the most up-to-date information on the most happening of places in Beijing, the reader is advised to eschew books in favour of the more flexible turnarounds of magazines and the web. See the restaurant reviews at *Time Out Beijing*'s website.

## Food

As a capital city and home to millions of foodies, Beijing is definitely the place to have the Chinese meal of your life. The relatively common distinctions of 'Peking', Cantonese and Sichuan food known in the West fall away before dozens of variations, including Mongolian barbecues, hotpots, dim sum, noodle bars, hot Hunan cuisine, 'Taiwanese' bakeries, tea houses, Shanghai sea food, Xinjiang restaurants serving Uyghur cuisine, and Yunnan exotica like fried bees.

As for 'local' foods, Beijing's various pasts as a deserted ruin or melting-pot capital have made it difficult for anything to be truly native. Even those foods traditionally regarded as 'local' by residents often turn out to originate in the tastes of the Qing dynasty's ruling Manchus, or the cosmopolitan new arrivals brought in by the Mongols. *Jianbing*, for example, the hearty, savoury pancakes that form a part of any Beijing breakfast, from hotel buffets to street-corner stands, are a Manchu import, as are the candied red hawthorn berries sold on sticks by street vendors, but both are now inseparable from the idea of Beijing cuisine, even among the Chinese themselves.

The food in the shopping malls is usually serviceable, albeit pricey by Chinese standards, but the very best restaurants in Beijing are the unassuming 'family' restaurants to be found a block away from the main streets, or at the edge of the hutongs. Do give them a go – I have never been disappointed.

One establishment that remains a permanent fixture is **Quanjude**, the self-proclaimed 'home of Beijing duck'. Certainly, if you are an aficionado of fowl, it is the place to have a succulent, juicy Beijing duck with sauces and shallots, as well as an entire table full of side dishes of duck dumplings, duck tongues, duck sausage... pretty much any kind of duck-related food you can imagine. Many fixed tourist itineraries seem to put in an appearance here or at the nearby **Da Dong**, and while they are perfectly nice restaurants, I personally find them pricey when similar dishes can be had for a fraction of the cost at many other places. Then again, I am not much of a fan of duck, and am usually regarded with snooty disdain when I show up with a party of foreigners and dare to order something duckless from the menu.

If you are the kind of person who wants to travel ten thousand miles just to eat a hamburger, then there are plenty of foreign food options in Beijing. The golden arches of **McDonald's** can be seen all over town; **Kentucky Fried Chicken** and **Pizza Hut** do a brisk business, and there are **Subways** for anyone who wants to experience the anguish of discussing ten different filling options in Mandarin. Chinese trendies are eager to sample exotic occidental mysteries like **Dairy Queen**, and Japanese franchises such as **Yoshinoya** are also found in abundance. The terms used for familiar products are crazily poetic – a Big Mac, for example, is a *Juwuba*, or an Immense Tyrant of Nothingness, and a Caramel Latte is *Jiaotang Natie* or Cook-Sugar Seize-Iron, but for the non-linguist, most fast food joints will have a pointing menu.

Local fast food chains also proliferate, such as the **Zhen Gongfu** Cantonese noodle franchise – 'True Kungfu', with its unmissable Bruce Lee logo. The **Dico's** chain, Taiwanese-owned but with a headquarters in Tianjin, is the largest local franchise, with thousands of outlets fit to match the number of McDonald's, and billing itself as a 'Western' restaurant, serving hamburgers, fried chicken and Chinese curries. **Li Xiansheng**, or 'Mr Lee', is an odd hybrid from the 1980s, set up in Beijing by the American-born Chinese Li Beiqi, serving beef noodle soup, and for that dash of foreign exotica, something called California Chicken. The chain used to trade on its Californian connections, but has become studiously more 'local' in its branding.

Chinese cookery is largely unforgiving of most dietary requirements. Buddhist traditions make vegetarianism a relatively widely-understood option, and even carnivores might like to try one of the dedicated vegetarian restaurants to experience the wonders that Chinese chefs can achieve with mushrooms and yams. The **Happy Cow** phone app can usually point the vegetarian at the nearest suitable restaurant in any given city. Otherwise, look for the character 素 (*su*), which literally means 'plain/simple', and has come to be associated with vegetarianism for its implications of austere living. Beware, however – tofu in China is not a substitute for meat, but often regarded as simply another legume; just because a dish has tofu in it, doesn't mean there is no meat to be found.

Halal food is also widely available in restaurants for China's twenty million Muslims, and is denoted by the characters 清真 (*qingzhen*), literally 'clear and true'. Halal restaurants can also usually be recognised by Turkic script on the sign, and often favour a green colour scheme. Uyghur restaurants are invariably halal, and the classier ones are not above putting on a show for Han Chinese clientele, so do not be surprised if the dinner crowd is serenaded by snake charmers and belly dancers. For a more authentic Muslim experience, try the night market or restaurants around the Niujie Mosque (see Gazetteer: Xicheng).

**Dini's**, 'Beijing's first and only kosher restaurant', can be found at the Central Chabad House (Gazetteer: Chaoyang), also home to a Jewish library with a small 'Sino-Judaic Museum' exhibit.

Exercise discretion with Chinese street food. Wok cookery and boiled noodles have evolved to disinfect the ingredients – but it's the cold treats and garnishes you need to watch for. Peel all fruit and discard the skins. One street food experience that you are liable to run into is the **Snack Street** just off Wangfujing (see Gazetteer: Dongcheng), which has dozens of kiosks and stalls, serving the usual Chinese snacks, alongside photogenically ghastly curios such starfish and seahorse kebabs. In the interests of research, I made my brother-in-law eat a deep-fried scorpion. He reported that it 'tasted like scorpion'.

## Drink

Guides at the Tap Water Museum (see Gazetteer: Dongcheng) insist that Beijing water is drinkable, at least when it leaves the source, and that any taint it accrues is due to the pipes it runs through before it reaches the faucet. Regardless, don't drink the tap water – boil it or stick to the bottled water available from any corner store.

Although few of his fans worldwide ever appreciated the meaning of the original lyrics, the Korean performer PSY lampooned the yuppies of Seoul's Gangnam district, who would eke out an existence all week on instant noodles, so they could be seen drinking an over-priced coffee at the weekends. His admonitions about this 'Gangnam Style' apply just as well in China, where middle-class professionals are bafflingly happy to pay for Starbuck's or Costa.

Beijing is riddled with Western-style coffee and cake shops, or Chinese-style teahouses – local favourites include **Pacific Coffee**, which hails from Hong Kong, and the **Chatime** franchise, which arrived in the 21st century from Taiwan. Such establishments take on a more bespoke quality up in the hipster hutongs around Nanluo Guxiang or Beihai North, the latter of which is home to numerous bars and cafés, almost universally sporting an earnest young Chinese man in a plaid shirt, strumming a guitar and singing about love and peace. There is a more riotous time to be found, particularly at night, in the Sanlitun area, a popular hang-out for many expats and Chinese rockers.

China is, of course, a tea-drinker's paradise, and one of the indis-putable bargains is tea itself. One of my most profound incidents of culture shock came in Fortnum & Mason in London, when I guile-lessly bought a packet of Iron Guanyin tea, only to discover that it was a hundred times the Beijing price. The tea-lover is hence urged to make at least one trip to a Chinese supermarket, where everyday teas are on sale alongside classier gift-packs.

## Alcohol

Although beer-like drinks have been brewed in China for thousands of years, the first modern brewery was built in 1900, in Harbin, by Jan Wroblewski, a Polish-German hoping to serve the Russian market brought in by the Trans-Siberian Railway. Captured by the Russians in WW2, but handed over to Chinese state control in 1950 during the Sino-Soviet love-in, the brewery's 4.8% tipple is now known as **Harbin Beer**, and can be found all over Beijing.

**Tsingtao Beer** has a name that similarly reflects its long pedigree – it has been brewed in the city of Qingdao since 1903, long before Pinyin Romanisation was invented. At the time, Qingdao was a German colony, leading to the production of a well-hopped, standard pilsner with 4.7% alcohol content; most Chinese beers, however, have a substantially lower alcohol content, around the 3% mark.

Tsingtao used to be the most popular beer in China, but was overtaken in 2008 by Xuehua, literally 'Snowflake' beer, often abbreviated as simply **Snow** or **Mons** (as it appears when written right to left), and founded in Beijing in 1993. Your correspondent finds it to be flavourless and gassy, and does everything he can to avoid being served it, by waiters who insist on explaining that it is the best-selling beer in China; there is no accounting for Chinese taste. Both Snow and Tsingtao are well-known all over China, while Harbin is harder to find in the south.

However, the beer you are most likely to encounter in many Beijing restaurants is **Yanjing Beer**, the product of a Beijing company founded in 1980. A State-owned company that uses the archaic name of the capital of the Land of Swallows, Yanjing Beer scored an impressive coup when it managed to get itself chosen as the official beer of State banquets at the Great Hall of the People. It is hence literally most likely to be found at Party parties.

Do not be surprised if you are warily asked '*Bingde?*' (Cold?) when you order your beer – there is a movement within Chinese traditional medicine that holds that beer at room temperature is better for you.

*Baijiu*, literally 'white alcohol' is a stronger, distilled spirit, usually hovering around 40–60% ABV, and made from sorghum, rice or other grains. Roughly equivalent to gin or vodka, it is China's traditional firewater, liable to put in an appearance at many a banquet. Chinese diners repeatedly toast each other, singly or in groups, on a number of pretexts, often denoting sincerity by an exhortation to *ganbei* ('drain one's glass', cognate with the Japanese *kampai*). For this reason, the size of the average *baijiu* glass has evolved into a manageable thimble – something to bear in mind if you bring some home. For the history of this most Chinese of tipples, visit the **Qianding Old Liquour Museum** at Gulou Dajie (Lines 2 and 8).

Modern times, particularly since the arrival of Chairman Xi Jinping and his austerity drives in 2012, have turned many trend-setting Chinese towards temperance, but *baijiu* remains a common sight. It is often exchanged as a gift by guests and hosts alike, leading to a fashion for ornate bottles and single-use packaging (even teetotallers are grateful for a posh box they can pass on with an unbroken seal), and concomitant price rises from the mere pennies for acrid Red Star *erguotuo*, to over £100 for a bottle of matured Kweichow Maotai. Call me a philistine if you wish, but the latter's high standing reflects cunning branding and association with high-profile opinion-formers, rather than any objective quality. *Baijiu* is an acquired taste at the best of times, but in my experience, the 'good' stuff turns up around the £15 (Y150) mark. Any cheaper and drinking becomes a test of endurance; any more expensive and you are likely to be paying for the bottle, and the fact that a pop star you have never heard of was seen drinking it last week.

The grape arrived in China in the Han dynasty, and flourished in the middle ages, although a millennium of Islam in the western regions led most of the crop to be processed as raisins until recent times. Modern wine production did not begin until 1892, when the Singaporean entrepreneur Cheong Fat-tze (a.k.a. Zhang Bishi) founded the Changyu company in Shandong, then a German colony. Since then, wine has had a chaotic development in China, beholden to substandard Eastern bloc grape varieties during the Communist period, before a sudden, steep and productive learning curve in the late 1970s. By 1998, most Chinese vineyards were shadowing, albeit not yet signed to, the code of oenological practice of the International Organisation of Vine and Wine, and Chinese wine production overtook spirits in 2001. Today, despite the relatively low standing of Chinese wine internationally, sheer demographics give China the largest wine-drinking population in the world, not only of local brands such as **Changyu** and **Great Wall**, but of foreign imports, many of which come from vineyards now part-owned by Chinese investors. Consumption remains a yuppie affectation, with local prices that often match those of imported brands, and a general cluelessness about such issues as refrigeration and decant-ing. However, the speed with which Chinese wine has gone from undrinkable to mostly harmless within the last decade suggests that it is on the cusp of a global transformation. The government certainly thinks so, and is already pushing for wine tourism and sales drives after 2017.

# 10

# Travel Logistics

CHINESE MONEY is the *Renminbi* (the 'People's currency'), although it is unlikely you will ever hear it called that, or even its other official name, *yuan* ('coin'). The colloquial term is *kuai* (a 'lump', originally of silver), and you will hear most sellers referring to [number] *kuai-qian* – literally 'lumps of cash'.

Market traders and junk shops often sell older versions of the currency, including the smaller *mao* denominations, adorned with attractive tableaux of minority peoples, or banknotes from the republican and imperial eras. Street sellers selling massive bundles of what appears to be counterfeit currency are actually selling 'ghost' money, to burn for one's ancestors.

Chinese pharmacies are plentiful and cheap, but unless you trust your own Mandarin-speaking abilities enough to explain what you need and read the instructions, bring your own supply of necessary medication. Even if you have a cast-iron stomach and avoid dangerous-looking foods, diarrhoea or mild discomfort can be a natural side effect of adjusting to new foods, so do not scrimp on the Imodium. As a rule, place no trust in Chinese ice cubes or condoms.

Foreigners used to be the lone nutcases wearing particulate masks to ward off the Beijing smog. Today, it is possible to buy masks at any corner pharmacy, and nobody is laughing any more. If travelling with children, you may prefer to get masks before travel, to save you the trouble of finding the right size when it is already too late. The author has never been troubled by the Beijing air, but if you are asthmatic or otherwise of a sensitive disposition, it is better to be safe than sorry. If you see a Chinese person wearing a face mask on a smog-free day, it is for your benefit – they have a cold, and are doing their best not to cough over everybody else.

## Getting Around

This book has been deliberately conceived with an eye to exploiting the vast expansion and convenience of the Beijing Subway, which now covers almost all of the sites liable to interest the foreign visitor. Although not quite idiot-proof, years of shepherding friends and relatives around Beijing has led me to regard it as a far more reliable mode of transport than the whims of bus routes, or the arcane symbols of addresses imparted to occasionally illiterate taxi drivers. Hence, most locations in the Gazetteer are given with reference to the closest subway station. Look for the tell-tale white-on-blue logo of a circle around the letter *D* – short for *Ditie*, itself an abbreviation of *Dixia Tielu* or 'Underground Railway'. The middle of the D is actually a solid B, for Beijing.

Except for the airport line, which costs extra, a single journey rarely costs more than Y6 – guidebooks published before 2015 make the excitable claim that it's a Y2 flat fee for anywhere in town, but this has been replaced by a sliding scale reflecting the much larger potential distances covered by the expanded lines. Make sure your map is also up to date – any guide more than a year old is apt to miss out entire stations or even lines. The *Yikatong* ('one card pass') card, available from kiosks at stations, can be charged with cash for multiple journeys, and does all the calculating for you. It can also be used in licensed taxis, and gives a 50% discount on the buses, too.

Beijing taxis remain convenient for visitors, although they can prove difficult to hail in rush-hour. Drivers cannot be expected to speak English; unless you are confident in your Mandarin, your first action on checking in should be to secure a hotel business card that has your address in Chinese, in order to ensure there is no confusion about where you want to go in an emergency. Similarly, although Uber is available for locals, it's best not to bother unless you are confident that you can explain down the phone to an increasingly fretful driver where exactly you are standing as he comes looking for you. Those visitors that require a taxi for the day can usually hire a driver for a flat fee of around Y600, subject to the usual haggling. Do not believe the surprising number of online tales of rip-off merchants – most turn out to be from newcomers who think they are being 'over-charged' because the driver also wants payment for the occasional Y10 road toll, e.g. to the airport or Badaling. If the meter is running, it is very unlikely that anyone is trying to swindle you – road tolls are not included in the metered fare, but also come with a receipt. Hotel concierges and airport security personnel are apt to write down the details of any taxi driver picking up a foreigner – this is to make it very clear to any potential wrong-doers that they literally have their number.

If you are planning travelling elsewhere in China, it's worth taking the time to register and familiarise yourself with the Ctrip website, which has an English-language interface but charges local Chinese prices for air fares.

## Security Issues

Sometimes, it may seem as if the centre of Beijing is populated almost entirely by soldiers and police. Tiananmen Square and its attendant attractions are the focus of any tourist trip for both foreigners and visitors from other parts of China, and are liable to be crowded with hayseeds who have just tumbled off the turnip truck and may require some careful crowd-control. The Square has been the site of several protests in recent years, usually taking the form of thrown paint or attempted arson. Coupled with the Square's iconic status and its past, both celebrated and suppressed, as a centre for political protest, the local security can be jumpy. This is not just about the chances of a random passer-by attempting a political statement, but the immense loss of face a young soldier is sure to incur if it happens on his watch. Walkman on full blast, I once narrowly avoided an incident, unaware that my child and I were blocking the path of an oncoming marching column of the People's Liberation Army, the leaders of which were too embarrassed to call a halt, and too terrified to use their rudimentary English to yell at me to get out of the way. I have also had many courteous but wary chats with soldiers asking where I am from, and why I am spending quite so much time skulking around.

It is standard practice for your Chinese hotel to take a photocopy of your passport on arrival. This is to register your presence with the local police and has no other sinister purpose. This saves the foreign traveller an immense amount of faff; if you are staying in a private residence, you are obliged instead to present yourself in person at the local police station within 24 hours, bearing your visa documentation and duplicate copies of your passport and visa.

Security guards are ubiquitous in China, and represent many levels of authority and jurisdiction, from humble doormen to the full-on public security police (*gong-an*). Many such jobs are sinecures or low-level appointments that simply work out cheaper in the long term than fences, pelican crossings or other permanent measures – don't be surprised to see officious old men in high-visibility jackets, standing on street corners, and blowing whistles in vain attempts to stop the Chinese jaywalking. In many public situations, they are apt to be terrified of you, since if the foreign stranger falls over, walks on the grass or transcends some other unspoken petty rule, it is the guards who will lose face, even though they are probably ill-equipped linguistically to tell you any of this. If they spoke a foreign language, they wouldn't be security guards.

## Shopping

One often suspects that the shopping malls of Beijing are merely putting on the performance of consumption, since many of them seem all but deserted, the L'Occitane and Hugo Boss franchises merely functioning as walk-in Situationist art exhibits. They are there in preparation for the much awaited 600-million middle class, or to whisper to passing Chinese what consumerist nirvana might mean if they ever have any money to spend. Prices are rarely notably cheaper than in the West.

That's not to say that there is nothing to buy in Beijing. Far from it, the city is awash with hawkers and pedlars, occasionally offering factory-fresh goods that have yet to enter Western consciousness. Shop where the Chinese shop, in the supermarkets and the shopping arcades, and there are bargains to be had. Wangfujing itself is something of a tourist trap, even for the Chinese – the locals are more likely to be found across town in the malls of Xidan (Line 1).

If the price is not marked, and sometimes even if it is, then it is not fixed, and you should feel free to haggle. Whatever the protestations of the seller that you are depriving his children of their dinner or robbing him blind, he is guaranteed not to sell you anything unless he is also making a suitable profit. 'Red' paraphernalia remains popular with both domestic and international tourists – the former liable to wear their Chairman Mao badges without a scrap of irony.

Shop around for silk and tailoring. The performance alone is enough to gain you better prices, since the knowledge that you are going to compare prices next door is sure to force a shopkeeper's hand. The better tailors in Dazhalan (see Gazetteer: The Centre) or the Xiushui Silk Street market (see Gazetteer: Dongcheng) will offer to knock up a suit or dress overnight, but will also appreciate the chance to make minor adjustments. Don't expect to pick up your suit at the last minute on the way to the airport; allow for an hour of faffery while they make the finishing touches that make them the best at what they do. This is particularly advisable if you have boobs, the sizes and variety of which outside China make every dress-making job a different kind of learning experience for the average Chinese tailor.

One consequence of the rise of the electronic book has been the collapse of English-language book sales in China. When every backpacker can carry a thousand digital volumes in their pocket, there is little incentive for stores to carry literature for the tourist market. Hence, English books in all but the very best stores are limited to language-learning materials and set texts (usually worthy classics) for the Chinese.

Consequently, there is little for the non-Chinese speaker in such heavenly, world-class bookshops as the multi-storey **City of Books** at Suzhoujie (Line 10). The best offerings for the visitor are in Wangfujing (Line 1), at the **Wangfujing Bookstore** and the **Foreign Languages Bookstore** – the latter is the author's favourite, and not only has a huge selection of books on Chinese subjects, but a floor dedicated to CDs and DVDs. The former did, too, at the time work began on this book, but by the time this book was finished it had transformed into a food hall, while the CDs and DVDs migrated upstairs to a smaller section. Things change fast in China.

Shopping for music elsewhere has also been hampered by the rise of digital distribution. Every supermarket has a CD section, but it is invariably stacked with nothing but that week's pre-selected hits, largely derived from whatever attention-hungry soubrette is taking curtain calls on *China's Got Talent*. Moreover, the shop assistants are usually passive-aggressively 'helpful', hovering briskly like hummingbirds at the sight of a foreign browser, and demanding to know what one is looking for. They genuinely seem baffled by the assertion that one is just looking to see what is actually there, suggesting that Chinese CD sales are driven solely by people who walk in already knowing what they want. There are occasional real music stores, even selling old-school vinyl, particularly dotted around the hipster hutongs – use them or lose them.

DVDs on sale in major stores are legal but usually coded for Region 6, hence requiring a multi-region player. A notable exception is the Red Cinema Classics series, many of which are region-free and come with English subtitles. You can't miss them – they're the ones that are packaged in a Blu-ray box, seemingly just for show. The author is unable to comment on Blu-ray availability in China, because no Chinese Blu-ray box he has ever bought has had a Blu-ray in it.

DVDs on sale on market stalls are usually illegal editions, ranging from freshly pirated Oscar nominees, still bearing the 'Property of the Motion Picture Academy' logo, to jerky home movies shot inside a cinema with so much coughing and disturbance, one can only assume it is somewhere in a hospital for the consumptive and incontinent.

Antiques, replicas, and bric-a-brac are on sale in a number of local markets. The biggest and most famous is **Panjiayuan** (Panjiayuan, Line 10, exit C), which began as an illegal yard-sale in a patch of woodland, and was eventually legalised and commercialised in 1995 as 'Beijing's First Antiques Market'. Use common sense with 'antiques', and proceed at most times on Aldrich's assumption in *The Search for a Vanishing Beijing* that whatever you're looking at is fresh off the factory line. Most items on sale to tourists will be replicas (i.e. fakes). The Chinese genius of fakery will sell you a facsimile of anything you desire – statuettes, pottery and jewels, often caked with an authentic layer of grime. True antiques are recognisable by a sudden ten-fold increase in price from a similar object. If you insist on the genuine article, also insist on a receipt, as without one you may be prevented from taking your dusty knick-knack out of the country. For this reason, you are advised not to buy 'antiques' from people in the street. Nor should you accept an invitation from an attractive 'art student' to come and look at a pop-up exhibition a block away, being run by her fellow daubers; this is usually a scam designed to push you into paying above the odds for sub-standard pictures and/or an unexpected outing to an overpriced teahouse.

Chinese airport personnel are often preposterously strict about cigarette lighters, to the extent of refusing to allow them even in checked-in baggage. So don't spend too much on that musical Chairman Mao lighter, as you may have to kiss it goodbye at the airport.

Some visitors to China will brag of electronic bargains. The best are actually liable to be found by staying in your hotel room and ordering stuff online for delivery to the front desk. For those who are unable to navigate the Chinese internet, the next best things are the shopping malls of Zhongguancun (Line 4), a development area riddled with glass towers and corporate sculptures, forming the Silicon Valley attached to several universities. However, browsing can be difficult, particularly if you don't know exactly what you are looking for, as concessions tend to be divided by brand, and salesmen can be pushy. Everybody is also quite savvy when it comes to the going rate online, so discounts are liable to be relatively small. There is more chance of saving money on second-hand or nearly-new goods, but in such cases do try before you buy to make sure you are getting the RAM or lens power you have asked for.

## Postage and Packing

Posting souvenirs home from China is considerably easier than doing so from many European countries. Small street-corner post offices do not carry international mail, although they might be able to sell you stamps for postcards. The main district post offices in Chinese cities have a packing counter, where a staff member will assess your goods, pick out a box and pack it for you. This not only saves you the bother of finding the materials yourself and puts your items in the hands of an artist with bubble-wrap and duct tape, but also helps you avoid any legal infringements. Chinese postal workers are sticklers for international regulations; if they refuse to pack something for you, it may be because of where you are sending it rather than out of any authoritarian directive. As the author discovered to his cost in Beijing, the *Finnish* post office regards ghost money as 'counterfeit', and hence will not permit it in parcels. Similar barriers often arise with regard to some of the more exotic foods you may wish to post home – you may be better off putting them in your luggage. Many countries are wary of fur products – if you have bought some, you may find that carrying them home is the safest bet.

Chinese postal forms require details of both sender (on the left) and recipient (on the right), as well as a rough summary of the three largest or most numerous articles in the package. They require five carbon copies, so write firmly and clearly, on a flat surface. Surface mail to Europe takes three months, but the service is reliable and efficient.

# II

# Gazetteer

'STUDY EVERYTHING AROUND YOU,' said the Sinologist John Bowring. 'Go out and walk in the street and read the shop signs. Bend over the bookstalls and read titles. Listen to the talk of the people. If you acquire these habits, you will not only learn something new every time you leave your door, but you will always carry with you an antidote for boredom.'

Beijing's museum-count took a sudden, exponential uptick during the approach of the 2008 Olympics, when the city government earmarked millions of yuan for the development of institutions commemorating every conceivable aspect of city life. In some cases, this led to the welcome restoration of derelict sites such as the Eunuch Culture Museum (see Gazetteer: Shijingshan), or quirky exercises like the Tap Water Museum (see Gazetteer: Dongcheng). A concise book such as this lacks the space to do justice to all of them, although the author would love to write a whole volume on just that subject.

The same period of hurried development accompanied a much more infamous bulldozing and demolition of much of the old city. Many of the old hutongs were destroyed in an orgy of reconstruction between 1997 and 2008. But you can still find a few, nestled behind the plate-glass facades of the shopping malls. Gold Fish Hutong, for example, and Dry Noodle Hutong, are a mere stone's throw from Wangfujing, while another nest of them encircles the Bell and Drum Towers north of the Forbidden City. Rickshaw-men offer 'hutong tours' of the more picturesque, but you may find your time is better spent wandering on foot.

The Chinese authorities have tardily come to recognise the heritage value of the hutongs, leading to several becoming protected areas.

While this has allowed a few nests of blue-collar workers to live close by to the toilets they scrub and the shops they staff, in most cases this has led to soaring gentrification – Rupert Murdoch and his then-wife Wendi Deng supposedly paid millions for a *siheyuan* house within spitting distance of the Forbidden City. Perhaps they hoped it would be handy for the buses.

The foreign visitor is apt to hear the term 'hipster hutong' applied to those areas of the most intense repurposing. Particularly around the Drum and Bell Tower districts, formerly squalid housing has been transformed into organic coffee shops, boutique restaurants and vinyl jazz emporia. **Nanluo Guxiang**, for example, runs north from the subway station that bears its name (Lines 6 and 8) towards the Bell Tower, and is riddled with cocktail bars, trendily 'Taiwanese' ice cream parlours, and the unforgettable sight of **Plastered T-Shirts** with its iconic, profane green llama in the window. Old China hands will sigh that the whole place has gone to the dogs – personally, I find it to be rather fun, and a handy shopping area to pick up that all-important vampire costume, model transforming robot and/or bobble hat with cat-ears. While it may not be redolent of the Ming dynasty, it is certainly a vibrant part of contemporary Beijing life, even for locals.

## The Centre: Tiananmen, the Forbidden City and environs

Built as a rival to Moscow's Red Square, and attaining much of its current appearance on the tenth anniversary of the People's Republic in 1959, **Tiananmen Square** is faced on its north side by the Forbidden City, on its west by the Great Hall of the People (site of the Chinese government), and on the east by the National Museum of China. Cars cannot stop on the main square itself, so do not be surprised if your taxi driver insists on turfing you out a block away. Although several Tiananmen venues are free to enter, they usually require identification, so don't forget your passport – on certain high-security days, you will even need it to get through the underpass to the square proper.

The central traffic island, so to speak, is itself the size of a park. Entrance requirements change periodically – on my last visit, the only way to the central area was through the underpass on the northeast side, where visitors must pass through another security check. Once in the centre, expect to find a few scattered kite-fliers and map-sellers, and a reverent queue for **Mao's Mausoleum** (open 08:00–12:00, Tuesday to Sunday). Leave bags at the left-luggage office, doff your hat, and expect to be turned away if you are inappropriately dressed. Although entrance is free, you will end up paying for left-luggage, and again if you want to rent some chrysanthemums to leave on the steps.

Often overlooked by visitors to the square is the tall obelisk of the **Monument to the People's Heroes**, surrounded by a series of bas-relief tableaux depicting eight crucial moments from China's wars of liberation, beginning with the burning of contraband opium in 1839, and taking in the May Fourth Movement and the War of Resistance against the Japanese in the 1930s.

On the south side of the square is the **Zhengyangmen** (Gate of the Zenith Sun, a.k.a. **Qianmen** or the 'Front Gate') – occupied by US Marines for a generation after the Boxer Rebellion. A compass dial on the ground beneath it marks the zero-point from which distances to Beijing are measured on all maps. Just south of it across the road is the **Arrow Tower**, another bastion. Tucked away on the south-east side is the former Zhengyangmen Railway Station, now a branch of the **China Railway Museum**. However, its central location, despite being inside an historic railway building, has little space for actual locomotives. If you want to see the trains themselves, you'll need to trek out to the main branch – see Gazetteer: Chaoyang.

The geographical heart of Beijing is the **Forbidden City**, also known as the Palace Museum or Old Palace (*Gu Gong*), a walled enclave where the emperors of the Ming and Qing dynasty whiled away their lives in a maze of maroon-walled, yellow-roofed palaces. Thanks to modern smog, it rarely has the aspect intended by its designers of a castle backed by the imposing, pagoda-topped hill to its north. It still feels somewhat like sacred ground – no subway line passes underneath it, and it is usually depicted in icon form on transport maps to mark the centre of the city. Beijing's first tram line once encircled it, hugging the walls – hence the naming of the first modern ring road, somewhat further out, as the 'Second Ring'. It is one of the last places in Beijing where pre-modern architecture and styles still have primacy and usually takes up at least half a day of any fixed itinerary. Owing to its significant role in both imperial and Communist history, it is a major destination for *Chinese* tourists, and you will have to pass through security gates to even get to the pavement in front of it. It is here, for some reason, a lot of drivers hand out business cards offering to take you to the Great Wall and/or Ming Tombs. Take one, as if you are unable to make alternate arrangements, they will get you there for half the cost of your hotel's concierge.

The Forbidden City's southernmost bastion, facing the square that has co-opted its name, is the famous **Tiananmen** (**Gate of Heavenly Peace**), where imperial decrees were once read out to the masses, and where Chairman Mao cannily chose to proclaim the foundation of the People's Republic in 1949. Pass through to find the entranceway and ticket offices, before proceeding, as thousands of loyal subjects have before you, to the grand courts, their flagstones worn down by uncountable feet.

The Forbidden City is, without a doubt, one of the most crucial sites on a once-in-a-lifetime tourist itinerary, but one suspects that for many foreign visitors it is little more than a succession of wind-swept courtyards. The historically minded should go the extra mile and hire a guide to explain the significance of each building. Humans are available, or rent one of the location-activated audio guides.

The Forbidden City rewards visitors who are prepared to take their time, particularly if they also take the opportunity to enter the many sub-museums and exhibitions tucked away in the alleyways and courtyards, but be aware, opportunities for food and drink are few once inside. There was once a Starbucks Coffee in the Great Within, but it was shut down in 2007 when even the Chinese found it to be a step too far.

The northern end of the Forbidden City comprises the former private residences of the emperors and their families, including the picturesque Imperial Gardens, as well as the rear exit. Beware, there is no turning back once you are out of it, and many an unsuspecting traveller has found themselves on the wrong side of the Forbidden City, with no cabs in sight, no idea which bus to take, no nearby subways, and no friends but the gaggle of eager rickshaw-drivers. There are subway stations to be found directly to your east, north and west, but all three are as far away as Tiananmen itself by this point – not good news if your feet are already tired from the walk.

The sole boon of being in this dead spot in the transport system is that you will be facing the entrance to **Jingshan Park** (Prospect Hill). More popularly known as Coal Hill, due to folklore that alleged it to be the site of a Qing-era fuel dump, this artificial knoll was actually made from the debris excavated in the construction of the lakes of Beihai Park. The British journalist Putnam Weale climbed it in 1900, and reported a popular myth from the period that the *entire hill* was made of coal, and intended as an apocalyptic booby trap and suicide device for the imperial family in the event of a foreign invasion.

> It was a long climb to the top, up winding steps that never ceased and through little pavilions that looked out on the scene below... Right below you could see far into the Palace and inspect the marble bridges, the lotus-covered sheets of water and all the other things of the Imperial plaisaunce. Father on, the city of Peking spread out in huge expanses hemmed in only miles away by the grey tracing of the city walls and the high-standing towers.

On a clear day, the view from the top is still the most awesome sight in town. Even in the smog, the Forbidden City looks haunting and ethereal – pound for pound, the Y2 entrance fee to Coal Hill easily trumps the Y60 ticket to the Forbidden City itself, at least for this jaded traveller.

At the base of the steps to the summit of Coal Hill is a pagoda tree, marked as the **Guilty Scholartree**. This marks the spot where the last Ming Emperor hanged himself in 1644, although the original tree was destroyed in the 1960s.

The east side of Tiananmen is the **National Museum of China** (admission free with a passport). The northern wing comprises the former Museum of the Revolution; the south is the Museum of Chinese History. The former is an excellent introduction to the story the Party tells itself about itself, not the least for the omissions, glossing over the Cultural Revolution in little more than a single photograph. For anyone in search of a swift march through China's past, the exhibits in the latter are well-chosen and suitably contextualised – the Terracotta Army, for example, is represented by a single exhibit, proportionally relative to the dynasty that spawned it lasting barely a decade.

Upper floors offer occasional exhibitions on particular artists, crafts or themes, such as a display of all the bonkers gifts presented to the head of state by foreign dignitaries over the years. You can imagine the look of utter disappointment on Hu Jintao's face when the Finnish president gave him yet another glass bird.

Just south of Tiananmen is the Qianmen shopping area, a heavily touristy street of international franchises, including Tissot watches,

Kentucky Fried Chicken, and a few faux-traditional tea shops. Just off the main drag, however, is the charming street of **Dazhalan** (the Great Stockade), usually garbled in local dialect as *Dashilar*. This street of shops, theatres and silk merchants judiciously preserves the flavour of the late Qing dynasty, when its location just outside the imperial enclave made it a flourishing trading post and arts community.

'Today we went into the Chinese City,' wrote Ellen LaMotte in 1916, 'and visited a native department store. At the best speed of our rickshaw boys we passed out of the [Qianmen], the principal gate, and once beyond the towering, embattled wall that separates the Chinese from the Tartar City, we lost ourselves in the maze of narrow, winding streets that open on all sides from the main road...'

Here, you can still find Yueshengzhai, a butcher's shop founded in 1830 (originally to sell left-over meat from sacrifices and divinations); Tianhuizhai, Beijing's very last purveyor of snuff; and the Daguan-lou, the very first cinema in Beijing, dating back to 1905. There's the Neiliansheng shoe shop (founded 1853), and guarded by stone *jilin* unicorns, the Tongrentang medicine shop (established 1669, moved to this spot in 1702), and the Duyichu dumpling restaurant (founded 1738), conferred with its name by its most famous client, the Qianlong Emperor. A street of more modern hawkers, selling the usual Little Red Books and furry hats, stretches north. Blink and you'll miss it, but a tiny alleyway leading away from this point is **Qianshi hutong**, former site of several silversmiths, reached by the narrowest alleyway in Beijing, in order to hamper the escape of any potential thieves. At its narrowest point, it is only 40cm wide.

While such curios attract many Chinese visitors, Dazhalan's main value to the foreign tourist is in its fabric and clothing stores. The most famous store is Ruifuxiang (founded 1893), and famous today as the supplier for the red silk used in the Communist flag first raised on the proclamation of independence. The street boasts several others, happy to sell fabric by the metre, or to rent out the services of their resident tailors. Overnight suit- and dress-making is possible, but the visitor allowing a few days may get a better price. Haggling won't get you very far, but demonstrating a readiness to compare prices will ensure that nobody is slapping on a surcharge just because you are foreign. Evidence suggests that the shops are not as 'in competition' as they might first appear, since several appear to share the same credit card machine.

Your mileage may vary – many old China hands decry Dazhalan as a sanitised, knowingly theme-parky rendition of old Beijing. Certainly, its olde-worlde charm has been very carefully managed; this was one of the first places in Beijing to embrace a sense of commodified heritage, instead of desperately demolishing everything old in favour of anything new. But I've been buying my shirts there for over a decade, and I still love it.

## Xicheng (West Central)

Pleasure garden for many an emperor, **Beihai Park** (Y20) is open to the public, unlike the Zhongnanhai lakes just to its south, which remain reserved for the Party elite. It is dominated by the **White Dagoba** built in 1651 to honour the visit of the 5th Dalai Lama – only one of several temples within the park's grounds. Look out, also, for the **Nine Dragon Screen** – built from glazed bricks in seven colours in 1402, and depicting the titular mythical beasts frolicking amid clouds and storms. Exit from the north of the park to find yourself in **Houhai**, the picturesque lakeside district that was once the northern terminus of the Grand Canal. It was, in fact, *so* picturesque that locals did seriously suggest that the 'View of the Mountains from the Yongding Bridge', in the middle of Houhai, should be substituted for one of the lost Eight Great Sights. These days, it's a rare occasion that you'll see the mountains at all, but look out for them, just in case.

Houhai is one of the most well-preserved of the hipster hutongs, retaining both old-world residential charm and new-age boutiques. It was once a sleepy district, only truly gaining its current nightlife and bustle since the SARS epidemic of 2003, when locals began to favour its outdoor tables and lakeside breezes over the close-quarters of Sanlitun bars.

As a former home for wealthy residents, Houhai comprised many larger mansions rather than cramped hutongs, and was home to several Chinese historical figures and celebrities, including the houses of authors **Lu Xun** (Y5) and **Guo Moruo** (Y20), **Soong Ching-ling** (a.k.a. Madame Sun Yat-sen, Y20), and the renowned female impersonator from the Beijing Opera, **Mei Lanfang** (Y20). For the uninterested tourist, to whom these are little more than names, time is better spent at the **Mansion of Prince Gong** (Y20), the best preserved imperial residence in the capital, and the former home of a one-time Imperial Regent. A son of the eighth Manchu ruler, Daoguang, Emperor of the Shining Path, and once considered seriously as a candidate for emperor himself, Prince Gong (1833–98) spent much of his life feuding and intriguing against his sisters-in-law, in particular the Empress Dowager Cixi. He tried valiantly to drag the imperial family into a realistic engagement with foreign powers, but was only posthumously recognised for his diplomacy and states-manship. Today, his house occasionally plays host to Beijing Opera performances.

Formerly known as the Garden of Ten Thousand Beasts from its days as an imperial menagerie, **Beijing Zoo** (Y15) is situated in pleasant parkland with plenty of room for human beings to wander, but sadly limited space for the animals themselves. This is a common factor in the layout of today's Chinese tourist sites, which are planned in anticipation of *millions* of visitors. For the traveller who is not heading to Sichuan, there is a small panda enclosure here – admis-sion is extra (Y5), but the ticket sellers usually assume that foreign visitors will want to go there, and automatically hand out the pan-das-included ticket unless asked not to. For some reason, guidebooks from many countries seem to imply that the pandas are in a separate zoo; they're not, they are within the main park. Parents of very young children may also wish to make use of the zoo's rather large outdoor playground – admission is an extra Y10, but there is plenty to keep the young visitor occupied, and the fee includes a handful of cabbage to feed to the nearby rabbits and ponies. Dogs are available for rental, for anyone who wants to... rent a dog. **Beijing Aquarium** (Y100) is also within the grounds, but requires a separate admittance fee. Note that the managers clearly do not trust the Chinese to obey the signs exhorting them not to feed the animals, so very little food is on sale within the zoo concessions that would trouble the digestive tract of a gibbon or giraffe. Bring your own lunch if you intend to stay for the whole day, or be content with pot noodles and popcorn.

It's all war, all the time at the **Beijing Military Museum** (admis-sion free with passport, closed on Mondays), which has its own stop on subway Line 1. There are numerous impressive displays, favouring China's turbulent 20th century, but also many historical conflicts.

The **Temple of the Origin of the Law** (*Fayuan-si*, Y10), founded by the Tang Emperor Taizong in 645 as a cenotaph for the dead of his ill-fated Korean campaign, can still be found near Caishikou station (Lines 4 and 9). As the oldest temple in Beijing, it was a natural choice in 1956 as the site of the Chinese Buddhist Academy, which is still based there. The site is close to the lively **Oxen Street** (*Niujie*), which is the heart of Beijing's old-time Muslim Quarter, and still boasts the city's oldest mosque, the **Niujie Qingzhen-si** (literally, Oxen Street Temple of the True and Pure, Y10).

## Dongcheng (East Central)

**Wangfujing** ('The Well of the Prince') is Beijing's most famous shopping street, although few of its malls offer anything that cannot be found anywhere else in the world – its meaning to the historically minded tourist is often tucked away in those places that seem at first sight to be nondescript and unremarkable. Wangfujing subway station (Lines 1 and 8) comes out at the huge **Malls at Oriental Plaza**, built by property tycoon Li Ka-shing in contravention of height restrictions designed to preserve the integrity of central Beijing's traditional buildings. You are supposed to be impressed because this is one of the largest shopping malls in Asia, as indeed you might be if you had been raised in a cave without access to Hugo Boss or Kenzo all your life. The plaza's most endearing feature is tucked away near the escalator at exit A of the subway – **The Wangfujing Palaeolithic Museum** (Y10) contains a one-room exhibition of the stone tools, bone artefacts and eggshells uncovered during the construction of the malls in 1996. Construction was delayed for eight months, and in a rare moment of heritage awareness for 1990s China, the finds were regifted to local government as the basis for this museum. It's almost the only reason for a foreign tourist to enter Oriental Plaza, unless you want to use the ATMs or have a desperate need to buy some Bose speakers. There are a handful of more interesting stores, such as **Shanghaixu**, which sells traditional dresses, and the embroideries on offer at **Emperor**, but most of the franchises will be familiar to you from far closer to home.

Many similar consumerist icons congregate along the broad pedestrian ramble of Wangfujing, and the visitor must look carefully to tease the historical elements from the everyday sights of familiar brands. This is not only because the giant signage of the Apple Store draws the eye far more readily than the unassuming manhole cover that marks the original '**Well of the Prince**' nearby, but because the march of progress has even doomed many of the 'new' arrivals, even as the caveman artefacts were preserved. Wangfujing was the site of Beijing's first McDonald's, the largest in the world in 1993, although that, too, was demolished in 1996 to make way for Oriental Plaza. The **Wangfujing Bookstore** was the biggest in China for many years, although its current location is immensely larger than the little boutique that held that position for so long.

Look closer at some of the less impressive stores to see evidence of their place in the history of shopping. The **Silian Hair Salon**, for example, comes spattered with gold plaques recording its heritage importance – it might be just a hairdresser's to you, but throughout the 1970s, this was the only place in Beijing where it was possible to get a perm, and even then, only if clients supplied documentation proving it was necessary for their work. Just as deceptively unremarkable, the **China Photo Studio** was once based in Shanghai, and was relocated to Beijing by government decree in 1956, whereupon it became the purveyor of photography to most government officials. Premier Zhou Enlai famously came to have his official portrait taken here, waiting in line with bus drivers and shopgirls, refusing to pull rank.

The **Arts and Crafts Emporium** was once the only place where foreigners were allowed to shop for certain Chinese souvenirs. These days it seems dwarfed by the bigger shops, although it still packs a lot into four floors, including folk arts, jewellery, and jade. More importantly, it also has the **Beijing Arts and Crafts Museum** (Y10), hidden away on its fourth floor, containing over 3,000 examples of the very best of Chinese embroidery, carving and other skills.

The **Underground City** (Dixia Cheng) has its entrance on Xidamocheng Jie, but has been suspiciously closed for renovations since February 2008, supposedly because of safety concerns.

There is another cluster of tourist sites up near Andingmen – the Gate of Pacification, through which all victorious armies would return. Famous enough to have its own subway station, the **Lama Temple** (Yonghegong, Y25) is a sanctuary of Tibetan Buddhism, boasting a huge statue of Maitreya and clouds of sweet-smelling incense. It also has the most high-tech admissions in town, since every ticket also functions as a CD-ROM giving further details of the temple's history. Nearby is one of Beijing's few surviving *pailou* – commemorative archways, familiar to many foreigner visitors from their duplicates in many a Chinatown. Once, such memorial arches were all over town, 'emblazoned all over with gilded characters and sprawling dragons, [to] honour some great Chinese – erected to his memory instead of a library or a hospital or something like that,' wrote Ellen La Motte in 1916. Almost all of them were pulled down in the next thirty years.

It's a short walk from there to the **Temple of Confucius** (Y30), admittance to which also buys the visitor a stroll in the grounds of the **Imperial Academy** next door. These twinned sites of scholarship are pleasantly bare of visitors and include several unexpected pleasures – there are concerts of classical Chinese music at certain times during the day, and locations are rich in history and folklore, such as the **Ink Lake**, a well from which scholars would drink in order to secure good fortune, and the **Corrupt Official Revealing Cypress**, a 700-year-old tree that once knocked the hat off a renowned charlatan. In the centre of the Imperial Academy is a gazebo from which the emperor himself would deliver an annual lecture, mumbling on a cosy throne about filial piety, while his words were bellowed in relay by a series of heralds to a waiting audience of 3000 people outside.

One of Beijing's hidden treasures is squirrelled away in nearby Guangximen (Line 13), on the third floor of the Institute of Fashion Technology. The **Museum of Ethnic Costumes** has lavish representations of most of China's minority communities; admission is free, but it is only open on Tuesdays, Thursdays and Saturdays.

Close to Yong'an Li (Line 1, exit A) at 8 Xiushui Jie is the **Silk Street Market** – once an actual market on a street, now a towering six-storey box festooned with advertising banners. It has floor after floor of boutiques crammed with clothes, bags, knick-knacks and fake designer goods, all destined to be yours after an energetic haggle. ATMs are on the first, second and third floors when you inevitably run out of cash. Silk and tailoring is on the third floor, but there is much more shopping to be had here.

The precise title differs depending on whether one is looking at a sign on the wall or the logo on the ticket, so you might call it the Beijing Water Supply Museum, if you so desire. Expats favour the **Beijing Tap Water Museum** (Y5) for the sheer oddity of the title, and although this institution does indeed boast a glass case full of bottles of water, it is a far more serious venture than the name implies. Just north of Dongzhimen (Lines 2 and 13), the museum occupies the location of the 1908 pumping house that first brought fresh water to the city's standpipes. It is here, at Dongzhimen, because this long-gone gate was the closest part of the city wall to the Sun River, from which the water was drawn. Exhibits tell the story of Beijing's troubled relationship with potable water, from early wells, to the attempts at modernisation, to the rationing of the early Communist era, to modern standards of purification and testing. The site is popular with local school trips, and it's easy to see why, because the smart historian can easily frame the last century of Beijing's entire history in terms of this unassuming little patch of land, where German guest-workers once constructed an ornate iron water tower (demolished and melted down during the Great Leap Forward), and Japanese occupiers, facing the drying up of the river, used a Hitachi pump to draw water up from an underground aquifer. Unfortunately, most of the signage is Chinese-only, and the earnest staff, while eager to impart their knowledge of water's path from source to faucet (in Chinese, *longtou*, or 'dragonhead'), only speak Mandarin. The linguist, however, may enjoy the implications of a bunch of historical exhibits that frequently parse attempts to push on through health scandals purely in terms of the spiffing new slogan that someone came up with.

Those in search of the echoes of the Boxer Rebellion will doubtless take a stroll through the avenues of what was once the **Legation Quarter**. 'When one speaks of the "Legation Quarter" in Peking', wrote Mrs Tweedie in 1926,

> ...one really means a great deal more than the Legations pure and simple, for there are many other things – banks, shipping agencies, photographic and druggist stores, kept by British, Germans, French and Americans. Book shops also, in fact everything and every trade is to be found in the Diplomatic Quarter. Each of the twelve Legations has its own large garden with its minister's house, houses for the doctor, councillor, secretaries and others, and their military guard.

There is, unsurprisingly, little recognition today of the Rebellion itself, tantamount as it was to state-sponsored terrorism, but you can still see many of the buildings of the foreigners' genteel little ghetto, mainly stretched out along the former Legation Street, now Dongjiaomin Xiang.

One of the foreign-built edifices, the old Citibank building, has now been repurposed as the **Beijing Police Museum** (36 Dongjiaomin Xiang, Y5), covering everything from the crime scene investigation practises of the Han dynasty, through to the adoption of modern innovations such as finger-printing and tasers. The fourth floor is given over to police weapons, and even has a laser-targeting range for budding cops. The exhibits on the 20th century are particularly interesting, documenting the rise of the Public Security Bureau (*gong-an*) since 1949, when policing Beijing and its armed militia, bandits and runaway warlords required considerably more than a truncheon and a loud voice. This is one of the few places in Beijing where the Cultural Revolution is given due acknowledgement, mainly because the PSB building was razed to the ground during the crisis.

In Qing times, the **Temple of Heaven** (Y35/Y15) was a vast compound just inside the walls of the 'Chinese' city, twice the size of the Forbidden City itself. It remains the largest area of parkland in the centre of town, and comprises a pleasant green area, dotted with trees, pavilions and the 500-year-old **Nine-Dragon Cypress**. The lower admission price is for the park; the higher one also gains you access to the multi-level altar where emperors would carry out their primary, primal function, as emissaries of the lands Under Heaven, beseeching the gods for a good harvest. A further Y10 buys you access to the Temple of Abstinence, where emperors would fast before the ceremony. Audio guides are Y40 with a Y100 deposit.

The 'morning bell and the drum at dusk' were common features of almost all ancient Chinese towns. In Beijing, the time was marked by Song-era water-clocks, and subsequently by the burning of more easily maintainable incense coils. The **Drum and Bell Towers** (Y15/Y10) are sited directly north of the Forbidden City, on the far side of Prospect Hill. Gulou Dajie (Great Drum Tower Street) was once one of the most thriving shopping districts in town, and today is a station on subway Lines 2 and 8; Shichahai on Line 8 is also within walking distance. Today, the Drum and Bell Tower district boasts many of Beijing's trendier boutiques.

The drums were struck quickly for 18 beats, then slowly for 18, in three rounds for a total of 108 beats, signifying not only that all was well, but that it was time to shut down the streets in curfew. The drum would then be struck every two hours to mark time through the night – one guide for scholars suggested a quick round of shadow boxing in the courtyard at the sounding of the midnight drum, in order to enliven the senses for further study. Author Xu Chengbei managed to find an old man in 2001 who remembered the sound from his childhood, associating it with the end of playtime:

I could hear the sound of the drum and bell every evening... The sound was agreeable yet awe-inspiring. I often heard such words: 'Stop messing about now. It's time to go to bed. Don't you hear the drum?' I rarely heard the midnight drum. When I heard it I was rather scared. I don't know why.

The bell would be rung, also 108 times, at seven in the evening and five in the morning. It was last used to mark time in 1924, when its chime was said to be audible for up to 20km. A modern experiment found it to be almost entirely muffled within a few blocks by the ambient clamour of modern Beijing.

Another site out of time, just outside the exit of Jianguomen station (Line 1 and 2) the **Ancient Observatory** (*Gu Guanxiang Tai*, Y10) features a garden and exhibition hall in the shadow of a blocky castle tower. Astronomical instruments from the 17th and 18th century, pilfered by German soldiers in 1900 but returned to China in 1921 in accordance with Article 131 of the Treaty of Versailles, now grace the rooftop and form baroque silhouettes against the plate-glass skyscrapers all around.

Close by is the **Ming City Wall Relics Park**, the only part of the old city wall to still be standing – and even then, only after substantial behind-the-scenes reconstructive help from modern concrete.

## Chaoyang (East Suburbs)

Beijing further to the east derives its name from Chaoyangmen (The Gate Facing the Sun), through which visitors would have to travel to get outside the city walls. The gate itself was demolished in the 1950s, and is now little more than a busy intersection of Chaoyang Road and the Second Ring Road.

Beijing's **Central Business District** is not central at all, but comprises a huddle of skyscrapers around Guomao subway station (Lines 1 and 10) on the eastern outskirts of what was once the old city. There is little for the tourist here, although many business visitors may find that they have been lodged here by their companies. The shopping malls sell the same stuff that is sold everywhere else, with possibly a little more emphasis on the needs of the expat community. A lot of embassy buildings are nearby, making some of the supermarkets homes away from home, selling rare delicacies like actual cheese. The area around **Ritan Park**, in particular, is practically a Russian colony, where the rickshaw drivers all hail you in Russian, and most of the buildings are adorned with Cyrillic. The rickshaw men get positively ratty if you respond in Chinese or English, so push your way through with a '*Nyet, spacibo*'.

The most distinctive geographical feature of the Central Business District is the CCTV building that sits at its edge. The headquarters of China's national broadcaster, this odd-shaped double-skyscraper, joined at the top, looks not unlike a pair of boxer shorts, and soon gained the local nickname *Da Kucha*, or the **Big Underpants**. Currently the tallest building in Beijing, and looking suspiciously like a Chinese knock-off of one of the ill-fated Twin Towers in New York, tower three of the **World Trade Center** has restaurants on its top floors affording a view of the city on a clear day.

One unexpected blast from the past, sitting there since 1319, is the **Dongyue Temple** (141 Chaowai Dajie), home to many effigies of Daoist gods and the **Beijing Folk Museum** (Y10).

Older guidebooks will make **Sanlitun** (Tuanjiehu, Line 10) sound like some sort of party paradise, as indeed it may have been back in the days when it catered to lonely embassy expats and the edgier among China's youth – it was supposedly the site of Beijing's first-ever Western-style bar, an unlikely claim considering the number of foreign hotels in the old Legation Quarter. While it still has dozens of little drinking tourist-trappy joints and cafés, the expansion of the city in the last decade has largely diluted much of what made it different. Sure enough, it has shopping malls all around, and boasts the '**world's largest Adidas store**', but to this visitor, at least, it looks like much of the rest of Beijing.

Once an out-of-the-way curio for the trendy art-lover, now swallowed up within the subway system (Gaojiayuan station, Line 14) and increasingly gentrifying to its detriment, the **798 Art District** is a former industrial zone, smartly repurposed into a warren of bespoke art galleries and cafés. Despite its recent addition to many a fixed tourist itinerary, and rising rents forcing out many of the young artists who gave it its cachet in the first place, it remains a good place to browse the work of some of China's newest creatives, and there are still bargains to be had.

Maps of Beijing show a perfect circle of railway track in the northeast of the city, past the Fifth Ring Road and not far from the airport. This is the China Railways test track, which also plays host to the **China Railways Museum** (Zhongguo Tiedao Bowuguan,

Y20), a hangar containing many locomotives and carriages from the country's tumultuous history with railways. It was once fiendishly difficult to reach (ironically for a site celebrating public transport), but the subsumption of the 798 area within the subway sprawl now makes an outing here feasible for the budget traveller. Pay the extra Y10 fee to get a look inside the private carriages of leaders like Chairman Mao and Zhou Enlai, to see how the elite lived in the good old days.

The massive, 65-acre **China National Film Museum** (7 Nanying Lu) is also close by, *within* the railway circle. Free admission gains access to over 20 exhibition halls, an IMAX cinema, and interactive exhibits about the history of the movies. The area is also home to the centre of Beijing's Jewish community at the **Bet Yaakov Chabad House** (Fanyuan Xi Lu, near the south gate of Si De Park), where one side of the library is also given over to a **Sino-Judaic Museum**.

Technically part of Chaoyang, although it is actually sited in the north of the city, is the **Beijing National Stadium** (Y50), better known as the 'Bird's Nest', built for the 2008 Olympics. Despite its impressive appearance and iconic status, it has struggled to pay its way in the years since – costing $11 million a year to simply maintain, and leading to a number of hare-brained schemes to attract customers when it is not hosting pop stars or lesser sporting events, such as its annual conversion into a ski resort with artificial snow from January to February. It is earmarked as the location for the opening ceremony of the 2022 Winter Olympics, at which point it will become the only venue to host both the summer and winter games. But the Bird's Nest is only part of a vast area of parkland and sports facilities, stretching all the way from Beitucheng station four stops north to Lincuiqiao – Line 8, which now reaches substantially further afield, was originally a special route for connecting Olympics traffic to the network. Some of these other attractions include the National Aquatics Centre (a.k.a. the Water Cube), admissions to which are a sliding scale from Y50 for a two-hour swim in the pool, to Y480 for VIP access to all the slides and treatments.

A couple of sites in the area are mercifully free of any sport – the **China Science and Technology Museum** (Y30), four floors packed with hands-on exhibits, although there is no guarantee all of them will be working at any one time, as it attracts a lot of local children running riot. Sadly, the signpost that once designated the **Ethnic Culture Park** (1 Minzuyuan Lu) as the 'Racist Park' has been taken down, although you will still see it on maps as the **China Nation-alities Museum**. Spanning two entire city blocks (there is a bridge across the road from the 'Tibet' enclosure), this intricate open-air exhibit crams 55 Chinese minorities into designated areas, each landscaped in imitation of traditional habitation. You can wander from Mongol yurts to a Manchurian palace to a Naxi long-house and all points in between, populated by performers who will burst into native song and dance at appointed times. The park's clearest landmark is a facsimile of a Xinjiang minaret, the Emin Tower, the real-world version of which still stands in distant Turfan. Consider-ing some of the disappointments of Beijing, the Y90 entrance fee is money well spent, and the site can serve as an instructive crash-course in the many subtle nuances of architecture that distinguish China's 120 million non-Han citizens from the majority.

Just south of the Ethnic Culture Park, **Beitucheng** subway station derives its name from the 'Northern Mud Wall' of the old Mongol city. The rampart is long gone, but its path is traced by a long, thin park and moat, stretching for three stops all the way to Xitucheng, the 'Western Mud Wall'.

## Fengtai (Southern Suburbs)

Deriving its name from the farms in proximity to Fengyimen, the Gate of Fitting Abundance to the old Jin dynasty Middle Capital, the 'Abundant Terraces' of Fengtai have now largely been swallowed up by urban sprawl.

Fengtai is the location of the architecturally awesome Beijing West Station, an 18-platform terminus for many of the trains coming in from the rest of the country, from the 21st-century bullet train from Shanghai to plodding overnight slowcoaches disembarking 3000km from their starting point in Hong Kong. For this reason, downstairs is chaos, although above ground it is an amazing sight.

The **Marco Polo Bridge** (*Lugou Qiao*, Y20) is now (just) within reach of the subway system, a short walk from Garden Expo Park station near the end of Line 14. As well as the bridge itself, now cross-ing little more than a meadow thanks to irrigation schemes sucking the water out of the river, the **Wanping Fortress** is worth a visit – climbing the walls costs Y5. This 17th-century castle, still bearing the scars of Japanese bombardment in the 20th century, is home to the **Museum of the War of People's Resistance of Japanese Aggression** (free). The brilliantly titled **Anti Japan War Sculpture Garden** is also nearby, along with a small market of hawkers selling grubby faux-antiques – feng shui compasses, silver dollars from the Republican era and the usual Mao memorabilia.

The Fangshan Line, which extends south-west from the very end of Line 9, is handy for reaching the **Western Han Tombs** at Dabaotai (*Xi Han Mu Bowuguan*, Y10), the graves of a prince and his wife from around 45BC. The same station is close to the **World Park** (*Shijie Gongyuan*, Y35), which offers scale models of many global landmarks for you to stomp through like Godzilla.

To see the **Peking Man** site (*Yuanren Yizhi*, Y30) in Zhoukoudian requires a substantially longer journey beyond the city limits to the south-west and is best attempted in a taxi hired for the day.

## Haidian (West Suburbs)

Once known as *Wadian* (The Swamps), Haidian got its more pictur-esque name-change to 'The Lakes' during the Mongol period, when it was the largest township to the northwest of urban Beijing. Like many outlying areas, it became both an entrepot for shops and ware-houses serving the city, as well as the location for businesses deemed unsuitable for the capital itself. In the 20th century, it gained a new cachet as the centre of the university district, home to Tsinghua and Yenching universities, and now many other colleges and faculties. Its association with high technology has also led it to develop something of a Silicon Valley reputation, particularly around Zhongguancun (see Travel Logistics: Shopping).

Built on the site of a prince's imperial garden in 1911 as Tsinghua College, **Tsinghua University** (between Wudaokou on Line 13 and Beijing University East Gate on Line 4) was the product of a plan by the US Secretary of State John Hay, and his president Theodore Roosevelt, to funnel $10 million of Boxer Indemnity money straight back into China as an educational resource. With two post offices, a hospital, schools and shops, it is a veritable academic enclave, whose students only occasionally venture into the outside world. The modern campus retains many features of its imperial origins, along with art installations and Edwardian architecture together with the more modern buildings. During the Cultural Revolution, it was also the site of fierce battles between student factions, although that is only briefly referenced in the University Museum.

Formerly the site of the Christian Yenching University (Yanjing University – named for the City of Swallows), **Peking University** continues the institutional memory of the former 'Imperial University', and like Tsinghua, boasts a campus rich in statuary and historical architecture.

These are only the two oldest universities in the Haidian district, which has accreted many other institutions of learning over the 20th century, including the People's University and the University of Agriculture. The **Beijing Aviation Museum** (Y4) is an odd curio, found on the campus of the University of Aeronautics and Astronautics (subway Xitucheng, Line 10), and featuring a large hangar full of interesting planes, as well as an upper storey that does its best to imply that China is substantially further ahead in the space race than it really is.

The **Old Summer Palace** (Yuan Ming Yuan, Y10) and **New Summer Palace** (Yihe Yuan, Y10) are both on Line 4 of the subway, the former at Yuan Ming Yuan Park, the latter at Beigongmen or Xiyuan. As discussed in Chapter 5, the old palace has been carefully left in ruins, while the new one has been tarted up considerably as a public park. Kunming Lake takes up some 75% of the area of the new palace, but be wary of succumbing to the temptation to rent a boat. On windy days, the breeze can build up significant force, and much more fun can be had watching the Chinese frantically trying to pedal or row against it.

The new Western Suburban Line stretches west from Bagou on Line 10, and incorporates two additional entrance points to the Summer Palaces, as well as several previously inaccessible tourist sites. Vandalised by Red Guards during the Cultural Revolution and still only partly restored, **Wan'an Cemetery** is the last resting place of Dong Haichuan (1797–1813), the founder of the Baguazhang school of martial arts.

Next stop along is the **Botanical Gardens** (Beijing Zhiwuyuan, Y10), not only comprising parkland, but the 'largest display greenhouse in Asia', the **Temple of the Recumbent Buddha**, a memorial to the novelists Cao Xueqin, and the site of Reginald Johnston's old vacation cottage, **Cherry Glen**. As with the Summer Palaces, the surfeit of interior sites can raise the cost of entry by Y50 or more, depending on what one intends to see.

The last stop on the line is **Fragrant Hills** (Xiang Shan, Y10), a 160-hectare park once used as yet another Qing-era pleasure garden, dotted with villas and shrines, and also containing the **Bright Temple**, a Tibetan lamasery that housed the Panchen Lama in the 18th century. The **Shuangqing Villa**, where Chairman Mao spent the summer of 1949, waiting his chance to take centre stage in the city below, is also here. The **Temple of Azure Clouds** (Biyun-si, Y10) is nearby, and includes a **Sun Yatsen Memorial Hall**, enshrining the first president of the Chinese republic, who died in 1925.

### Shijingshan (Western Hills)

'As one approaches the capital city,' wrote the former US ambassador Paul Reinsch in 1922, 'the beautiful mountain forms of the so-called Western Hills, which rise suddenly out of the plain about ten miles beyond Peking and attain an altitude of from six to seven thousand feet, present a striking contrast to the flat and far-stretching Chihli plain.'

Once known chiefly for the Jade Spring (Yuquan), from which a convoy of carts would bring daily replenishments for the imperial household's water supply, the 'Western Hills' technically include some of the temple complexes and parkland now incorporated within Beijing's western suburbs (see Gazetteer: Haidian). It only shows up as a small area on the tourist map of Beijing, although the mountains extend much further – Dragon Bone Hill, site of distant Zhoukoudian (see Gazetteer: Fengtai), is part of the same range.

It was once a site for expatriate hikes and picnics, as recorded by Ellen LaMotte in 1916. 'Below us spread a magnificent vista of more hills, a great, far-reaching panorama, with the old Summer Palace in the distance. In all directions we could see temples perching on the distant hills...'

Unfortunately, although the Western Hills retain some parkland, and are gradually being rewilded to a more pleasant appearance, the area spent much of the 20th century as a drab industrial zone, complete with factories and smoke-belching power stations. The grand vistas recounted by visitors of a century ago are largely a thing of the past.

Despite its distance from the centre, the area was one of the first to be incorporated into the subway system, thanks to the presence of a large military complex below ground – Line 1 continues after Pingguoyuan for two further stops, closed to the public, partly for military security, and partly because students from the nearby Mass

Transit Railway Technical School use the quiet section to practice their train-driving. These phantom lines take the tracks right through the Western Hills and out the other side, where they connect again with the public network at Sanjiadian. Actual public access through the subway network is finally possible through several newly completed extensions that pick up where Lines 1 and 6 leave off, and head up into the hills.

The Tomb of Tianyi (*Tianyi Mu*), better known as the **Beijing Museum of Eunuch Culture** (Y8), is a fascinating site. Despite forming a crucial part of the social structure of Chinese imperial life, the eunuchs of the palace were rarely commemorated or remembered, a fact addressed by displays recounting the history of the creation, lives and deeds of many of China's historical eunuchs, maintained on the site of the grave of Tianyi (1534–1605). As well as grisly dioramas, there are exhibits taken from the possessions of Sun Yaoting (1902–1996), the last eunuch to serve the Last Emperor. It is also possible to take a creepy journey into the barely-lit shadows of Tianyi's tomb, looted in the 1920s. The nearby **Fahai Temple** (Y20/Y100) is famous for its Buddhist wall paintings, although the lower of the two entrance fees only buys you access to their modern replicas. Both are within walking distance of Jin'an Qiao subway station (Line 6).

Fushouling, once intended as the final stop of Line 1, now rebranded as a station on the new Yuquanlu extension that branches out from Tiancun on Line 6, is the closest station to **Badachu**, the 'Eight Great Sites'. Alternatively, take the 972 bus from Pingguomen station (Line 1). Not to be confused with the Eight Great *Sights* (see Chapter 4), this hilly parkland is the location of several temples and holy buildings, including the **Temple of Eternal Peace** (Chang'an-si), the **Cave of Precious Pearl** (Baozhudong), and the **Dragon Spring Nunnery** (Longquan-an). Admission is Y10, although it costs Y50 for a cable car to truncate the journey, and a further Y3 for the questionable merit of seeing **China's Largest Inkstone**. The view from the top encompasses all of Beijing, but *only on a clear day*. Good luck with that.

## Further Afield

Usually known in Chinese simply as the 13 Tombs (*Shisan Ling*), the **Ming Tombs** were once a day's ride outside the city – a final resting place for all the emperors of the Ming dynasty from Yongle's time to its end. Today the site is the terminus on the Changping Line that branches from Xi'er Qi (Line 12), about an hour from the centre of town. The necropolis stretches for miles along the foothills of the mountains, but while it is rewarding for hikers to wander among the many pavilions and tumble-down monuments, only a handful of the sites are technically tourist-friendly.

Although every tomb has a 'Sacred Way' (Y30) approach-road, the first, largest and best is that which is pointed directly at **Changling** (Y45), the tomb of the Emperor of Perpetual Happiness. It's worth a stroll along its 7km of statuary – the pathway that the descendants of Yongle were expected to take on their way to honour him in the after-life. The tomb itself is not open, but the courtyards and pavilions of his temple buildings make for a pleasant, if dusty, museum of his life.

To the west is **Dingling** (Y60), the tomb of Wanli, Emperor of 10,000 Experiences (1563–1620). Open to the public, this was the site of an ill-fated archaeological excavation in the 1950s, which rushed ahead without adequate measures in place to preserve the lavish silk garments and hangings to be found inside the tomb, many of which were left to rot in a damp shed. Matters were compounded by the outbreak of the Cultural Revolution, which not only suspended archaeological work, but culminated in the invasion of the site by fanatic Red Guards, who dragged out the skeletons of Wanli and his concubines, denounced them as if being dead were not punishment enough, and then set fire to them and their possessions. Despite such atrocities, Dingling is worth a look for the opportunity to venture below ground into the 'underground palace' of the tomb itself beneath the grave mound.

Also open to the public is **Zhaoling** (Y30), tomb of Wanli's father Longqing (1537–72), the Emperor of Grand Celebration, which is the most complete and undamaged mausoleum extant at the site. Of the other sites of the necropolis, a hiker can spend a happy day wandering the ruins. If I had to pick one, it would be the one that is actually on the other side of the river, off to the west of the main Sacred Way. It is far less impressive on the outside, because it was never intended to hold the body of an emperor. **Siling** was originally built to hold the body of a favourite concubine of Chongzhen, the Emperor of Lofty Omens (1611–44). This was that same unfortunate Ming ruler who presided over the country's multiple crisis of crop failures, famine and foreign invasion, and who hanged himself, aged 33, at the foot of

Coal Hill as the soldiers of Li Zicheng marched into town. After the emperor's death, he was hastily interred in this humble spot. Touchingly close by is a memorial tablet to Wang Cheng'en, his most loyal eunuch, who followed his master in suicide. Siling makes for a melancholy coda to the majesty of the Ming dynasty – in comparison to the palatial tomb of Yongle nearby, it is little more than a pauper's grave.

The other famous site outside Beijing city limits, of course, is the Great Wall itself, or rather, those sections of the Ming dynasty fortifications which are close by. The nearest and most heavily populated section is **Badaling** (Y45, cable car extra) – not quite inside the subway network, but only an hour's train ride away out of Beijing North station, for a mere Y6. Many travellers prefer to make a day of it on the bus or with a hired taxi – the latter is by far the better option, as it reduces the chances of unwanted 'detours' to look at someone's cousin's jade factory or other tourist traps. Day trips and other fixed itineraries tend to head out to the wall and then stop in at the Ming Tombs on the way back. Such an itinerary is also possible with a wall trip to the vertiginous drops of **Juyongguan** or the newer wall site further afield at **Mutianyu** (Y45, cable car extra). In all cases, the smart tourist gets to the wall *early* – even the outer sites fill up with tourists after midday.

There are many other sites on the Great Wall, but the other one liable to attract the notice of tourists from Beijing is **Simatai** (Y40). Too far out to be anything but a single destination for the day (it's three hours by car or bus), Simatai has recently been remodelled to include Gubei 'Water Town' (www.wtown.com), an old-world reconstructed hamlet of canals and lakes, linked by picturesque bridges and boasting of boutique restaurants and local artisanry. It's worth the trouble if the visitor's itinerary is not going to include trips to similar enclaves in Shanghai or Hangzhou – there is a hotel on site if you prefer to arrive late in the day and be up ready for the wall *really* early.

One more journey worth considering away from Beijing, should you have inexplicably tired of it, is to the nearby city of **Tianjin**, a mere 33 minutes away by bullet train. But that's another book.

# Chronology of Major Events

**BC**

| | |
|---|---|
| c.500,000 | First arrival of *Homo erectus pekinensis* in Zhoukoudian. |
| c.400,000 | Evidence of Upper Cave Man (Homo sapiens) at Zhoukoudian. |
| c.25,000 | Deer hunters camp on what is now Wangfujing. |
| c.2000 | Bronze tool working in the Beijing area. |
| c.1200 | Establishment of a walled city, *Yanjing*, Capital of the Swallows. |
| c.105 | The Land of Swallows is a dukedom pledging fealty to the king of the Zhou dynasty in the south. |
| 323 | Duke Yi of the Yan (the Land of Swallows) proclaims his own kingship, throwing off the authority of the Zhou kings. Beginning of the area's century as an independent state. |
| 318 | King Kuai of Yan abdicates, giving his throne to his chief minister Zizhi. |
| 315 | Civil war and occupation by Qi (the Land of the Devout). |
| 312 | Withdrawal of Qi forces. Zizhi is deposed. |
| 284 | Yan army invades and occupies the Land of the Devout, led by Yue Yi. |
| 283 | Construction of a wall to mark the north of Yan's borders. This would later be incorporated within the first 'Great Wall'. |
| 232 | The Red Prince returns to Yan without the king of Qin's permission. |
| 231 | Presumed commencement date of the Red Prince's assassination plot. |

| | |
|---|---|
| 227 | Jing Ke's assassination attempt on Ying Zheng, the King of Qin, masterminded by the Red Prince. |
| 226 | Qin forces storm the Land of Swallows in retaliation, forcing the Red Prince's father to flee north-east to Liaodong. |
| 222 | The last of the Yan defenders is defeated in Liaodong; official date of the fall of Yan. Surrender of King Xi. |
| 221 | Having conquered every rival state, the King of Qin proclaims himself to be the First Emperor of China. |
| 215 | The First Emperor visits the former Land of Swallows. |
| 209 | With the collapse of the Qin dynasty, the Land of Swallows is briefly independent once more. |
| 202 | The Land of Swallows is brought back within the empire, subsumed within the domain of the Han dynasty. |

**AD**

| | |
|---|---|
| 25 | The former Land of Swallows is the power base for Liu Xiu, who subsequently becomes the first emperor of the Eastern Han dynasty. |
| 250 | Commencement of major water engineering projects in the area, designed to improve irrigation. |
| 294 | Local inhabitants, even foreign immigrants, pool their resources and labour to repair flood and earthquake damages in the region. |
| c.300 | The city is renamed *Youzhou* – the Tranquil City. |
| 314 | The region falls unde rthe influence of non-Chinese races, including the Xianbei and Toba – both regarded by the Chinese as 'barbarian' races. |
| 337–370 | State of Former Yan |
| 384–409 | State of Later Yan |
| 384–394 | Western Yan |
| 398–410 | Southern Yan |
| 409–435 | Northern Yan |
| 607 | The region is linked by a canal with the south, brought back within the orbit of 'Chinese' rulers. |
| 611 | Youzhou is a staging post for armies of the new Sui dynasty for attacks on Korea. |

| | |
|---|---|
| 644 | The Taizong Emperor of the Tang dynasty returns to Youzhou in an attempt to complete his predecessors' military actions. |
| 645 | Taizong builds the Temple of the Origin of the Law, a cenotaph in memory of Chinese soldiers fallen in Korea. |
| 755 | The city is a major base in the rebellion of An Lushan against the Tang dynasty. |
| 759 | A local attempts to proclaim a Yan 'dynasty', but fails. |
| 917 | Early incursions of Khitan tribesmen. The region is largely depopulated as Chinese colonists flee south for their own safety. Slow commencement of three centuries of North-South division. |
| 1025 | Only a couple of generations after their arrival, the Khitan rulers have been sufficiently sinicised to want to imitate the Chinese in the south. Examinations and sacrifices in Yanjing follow Chinese traditional models. |
| 1115 | The Jurchen tribesmen of the hinterland proclaim a new 'Chinese' dynasty, the Jin or 'Golden'. |
| 1120 | The emperor of the Song dynasty unwisely attempts to oust the Khitans by arranging a deal with the Khitans' Jurchen rivals. Instead of restoring the region to the Song, the Jurchen take it for themselves. The city becomes Zhongdu, the 'Middle Capital' of the Jin. |
| 1192 | Completion of the 'Marco Polo' Bridge. |
| 1211 | First Mongol attack on Zhongdu. |
| 1215 | Fall of Zhongdu to the Mongols. |
| 1266 | Khubilai Khan orders the reconstruction of Zhongdu. Extensive remodelling of the water system. The city is renamed *Dadu* or *Taidu*, the Great City. |
| 1275 | Arrival of Marco Polo in China. He writes of Dadu as *Cambaluc*, thought to be his transliteration of the Turkish Khanbalik – 'the Khan's City'. |
| 1293 | Completion of the new canal link to the south. |
| 1345 | Famines and floods lead to anti-Mongol unrest. |
| 1368 | Mongols driven out of China by the new Chinese Ming dynasty. The city is renamed Beiping – 'Northern Peace'. |
| 1371 | Extensive reconstruction in Beiping, as the administrative centre of the emperor's fourth son. |

| | |
|---|---|
| 1402 | The fourth son of the late emperor seizes the throne, proclaiming himself to be Yongle, the Emperor of Perpetual Happiness. He relocates the capital to his own power base, and Beiping is renamed Beijing – Northern Capital – for the first time. |
| 1530 | Construction of the altars to the Sun, Moon and Earth. |
| 1601 | Arrival of Matteo Ricci, a Jesuit missionary, in Beijing. |
| 1644 | Beijing is captured by the armies of the Manchus. The last Ming emperor hangs himself from a tree on Coal Hill, north of the Forbidden City. |
| 1648 | All Chinese residents are banished from the inner city of Beijing, which becomes a sector reserved exclusively for Manchus. |
| 1694 | Russian community in Beijing begins to grow. |
| 1745 | Early work begins on the gardens of the Summer Palace. |
| 1793 | Visit by the first British ambassador to China, George Macartney. |
| 1831 | Flooding near the Marco Polo Bridge. |
| 1896 | Completion of the first railway between Beijing and Tianjin. |
| 1900 | The Boxer uprising and the subsequent occupation of the city by foreign troops. |
| 1902 | Cixi, the Empress Dowager, returns to Beijing by train. |
| 1912 | Abdication of the Last Emperor. |
| 1916 | Yuan Shikai fails in his bid to become the first emperor of a new dynasty, and dies later the same year. |
| 1919 | Events at the Paris Peace Conference lead to the May 4th demonstrations in Beijing. |
| 1920 | First Chinese Communist organisation founded in Beijing. |
| 1928 | Nanjing is the capital again. Beijing renamed Beiping. |
| 1937 | The Marco Polo Bridge incident sees the first shots fired in the Second Sino-Japanese War. |
| 1938 | Japanese occupy Beiping and rename it Beijing once more. |
| 1941 | Japanese attack on Pearl Harbor. US and British residences in Beijing are occupied by the Japanese military. |

1945    At the close of the Second World War, Beijing is contested between Chinese Nationalist and Communist forces.

1948    Communist forces surround Beijing.

1949    Surrender of Nationalists in Beijing. Chairman Mao proclaims the foundation of a new Communist state – the People's Republic of China.

1959    The tenth anniversary of the PRC sees central Beijing remodelled with Soviet-style architecture and a wide open space in front of the Tiananmen gate.

1968    The army is deployed in Beijing in order to quell fighting between rival factions of Red Guards.

1971    Construction begins on the Beijing subway.

1972    Richard Nixon visits China.

1976    Death of Chairman Mao. His mausoleum is built in Tiananmen Square.

1985    Rioting in Beijing after the home team loses a soccer match against Hong Kong.

1986    Queen Elizabeth II visits China.

1989    Student demonstrations in Tiananmen Square are suppressed with tanks.

1990    Beijing hosts the Asian Games.

1993    Failed bid to hold the 2000 Olympics.

2001    Beijing's bid to host the 2008 Olympics is successful.

2003    SARS epidemic encourages outdoor drinking – close-packed Sanlitun bar culture begins to wane in favour of Houhai cafés.

2008    Beijing Olympics.

2013    Beijing pollution levels officially proclaimed 'hazardous to human health'.

2014    Power station shutdown for the APEC conference leads to the new slang term for skies improved by politically motivated beautification: 'APEC blue'.

2022    Winter Olympics opening ceremony to be held in Beijing. President Xi Jinping promises it will be 'fantastic, extraordinary, and excellent.'

# Further Reading and References

A T THE TOP OF WANGFUJING, opposite the Foreign Languages Bookstore, there is a bronze statue of a gaunt Qing-era peasant pulling a rickshaw. The seat is empty so that passers-by can be photographed in it, and the pulling poles have a gap in them to afford easy access. Not a minute goes by without someone clambering in for an opportunistic selfie, but there is much more to the statue than that.

The statue's name is *Xiangzi Pulling a Rickshaw*, and it commemorates Lao She (1899–1966). His best-known novel, published variously as *Rickshaw*, *Rickshaw Boy* or *Camel Xiangzi* is a satirical account of a wheeler-dealer in 1930s Beijing, who hopes to climb the social ladder by first renting, and then buying a rickshaw. Xiangzi has very little luck – he is bitten by a donkey as a child, he is swindled by his customers and victimised by the authorities, and his toils come to nothing when his beloved rickshaw is stolen in an allegory of the false promise of capitalist dreams. That is only the beginning, as he moves into the potentially more lucrative world of camel droving, and beyond. But Xiangzi is not merely a satirical character, he is a passionate Beijinger, deeply reluctant to leave the city that has raised him: 'filthy, beautiful, decadent, bustling, chaotic, lovable' Beijing. His fate was rewritten in the Communist era, when Lao She was persuaded to tack on an ending more suitable for the Communist utopia of 1949.

Lao She himself was not so lucky, hounded to his death during the persecutions of the Cultural Revolution. His body was found floating in Taiping Lake, but not even that is there any more – it was filled in some years ago, and now it is just another street, up near the Second Ring Road, near an orthodontic hospital and a subway drivers' dormitory.

## Guidebooks

Taking a guidebook should no longer be a matter of fretting over space and weight, since all major versions now offer e-book editions. However, the e-book format is not the best way of dipping in and out of a large tome, and the smart reader may prefer to take a chunky China guide from Lonely Planet or the Rough Guides in digital form, and a sleeker, more portable Beijing guide in paper form from Insight Flexi-maps or DK Eye Witness. Those who rely on their phone for mapping and global positioning may discover that the Great Firewall suddenly cuts them off. Make sure you have a local back-up.

Unless otherwise noted, all the sources listed here are in English. I have, however, also made use of some foreign-language accounts in order to get a sense of how Beijing looks to other visitors. Some of my ideas and approaches have leaned on the Chinese tourist guide *Beijing Gonglüe,* literally 'Tackling Beijing' (Posts & Telecom Press, 2013) and the ever-valuable Japanese-language 'Rurubu' guidebook *Pekin* (JTB Publishing, 2011).

For the chance to see what has changed since your last visit, and what events are happening this very week, as well as the most up-to-date map, pick up one of the free *Time Out City Guide* folding maps, usually to be found right next to the airport taxi rank, and well worth a look, no matter how many times you have been to Beijing before. See also the websites for *Time Out Beijing* and *That's Beijing,* the online presence of which are packed with restaurant reviews, party planners and articles on what's really, *really* new.

## General Accounts

There are several excellent books about Beijing and its history, including Stephen Haw's *Beijing: A Concise History* (Routledge, 2007) and M.A. Aldrich's *The Search for a Vanishing Beijing: A Guide to China's Capital Throughout the Ages* (Hong Kong University Press, 2006). Aldrich is rich in anecdote and trivia, and displays a *flaneur*'s eye for Beijing life. He is also the author of an unexpectedly detailed history of Beijing told entirely from the point of view of the experiences of its Muslim population. Featuring photographs by Lukas Nikol, his *The Perfumed Palace: Islam's Journey from Mecca to Peking* (Garnet, 2010) is a captivating exercise in telling a familiar story through an unfamiliar framework.

For a real sense of the gritty, slippery reality of chronicling the city's many rises and falls, Jasper Becker's *City of Heavenly Tranquillity: Beijing in the History of China* (Penguin, 2008) is highly recommended, not the least for its scathing account of the destruction of the old city since 1997.

In the early years of the 21st century, Mao Xiang was a guide offering walking tours to foreign tourists. Although he has now relocated to Canada, his legacy lives on in *Beijing Walks: Like a Flying Feather Through the Hutongs* (Foreign Languages Press, 2012), a 471-page compilation of 16 historical tours of the city. Reprinting his notes to what appears to be an exacting degree – second-person asides, restaurant tips and all – this idiosyncratic book contains a wealth of historical information, adding unexpected depth and insight. Born and bred in the hutongs, Mao plainly mourns the loss of many landmarks, although his book was published at a fortunate time when the destruction of the old city was finally curtailed, and hence remains up-to-date – if there is one book worth buying *in* Beijing, this is it.

For a real insider's eye view, Liu Aifu's *English Tour Guiding in Beijing* (China Tourism Publishing, 2014) is an absorbing English-language textbook for would-be guides, giving them all the details they are likely to need while shepherding foreigners around. As one might expect, certain modern topics are conspicuous by their absence, but it's particularly good on the big sites like the Forbidden City and the Temple of Heaven. It also has an unexpectedly intriguing troubleshooting chapter on such matters as what to do if one of your clients dies mid-trip.

Somewhat haphazardly translated, such that one often needs to speak Mandarin to actually understand it, Liu Baoquan's *Beijing Hutong* (China Travel & Tourism Press, 2008) is a toponymic study of Beijing, concentrating on the evolution (or as it would have it, the 'evolvement') of the various place-names. There is much fun to be had here, in the historic euphemisms shunted onto places once known as Donkey Meat Alley or simply Doghole – the mind boggles. Look here for glimpses of Beijing's past, and trivia about the name-origins of many streets and stations, and the complex historiography of the word *hutong* itself. For the true completist, the book also includes a nine-page list of Chinese celebrities, everybody from the Last Emperor to Li Hongzhang, and their one-time hutong addresses.

Xu Chengbei's *Old Beijing: In the Shadow of Imperial Throne* (Foreign Languages Press, 2001) is often frustratingly apocryphal or uncritical, but contains valuable slice-of-life sections, pictures, and anecdotes not repeated elsewhere.

## Publishers and Authors

Hard to find outside China, but readily snapped up at the Foreign Languages Bookstore (see Travel Logistics: Shopping) are a number of bilingual guide books by the Beijing Art Photography Press, now part of the Beijing Publishing Group (somewhat counter-intuitively abbreviated as BPH), and useful both for the researcher and souvenir hunter. Titles from the likes of the Foreign Languages Press are also a bargain in China, whereas they are often sold abroad at a hefty mark-up.

It is difficult to choose representative Chinese authors from among the many thousands who have written about Beijing. The aforementioned Lao She is one of the city's most famous sons, and the most recent of many translations of *Camel Xiangzi*, Howard Goldblatt's *Rickshaw Boy* (Harper Perennial, 2010), remains mordant and insightful. Its account of the young men who 'mortgage their youth' in pursuit of nebulous success, with the odds weighed against them, still speaks to the daily lives of the taxi-drivers, shopgirls and yes, even rickshaw men who still ply their trade in Beijing.

Any investigation of modern books about Beijing must wade gingerly through entire shelves of self-indulgent, lazy *romans-a-clef* by hateful twentysomethings, in which charmless ciphers only look up from their smartphones to complain about their lattes. This, too, is a faithful glimpse of contemporary Beijing life, albeit no fun to read. However, a few modern novels have inherited some element of Lao She's soul, such as Yan Geling's *The Banquet Bug* (Hyperion, 2007) published in the UK as *The Uninvited* (Faber, 2007), in which a ne'er-do-well discovers he can eat like a prince as long as he poses as a journalist at public functions. Similarly, Xu Zechen's *Running Through Beijing* (Two Lines, 2014), lionises an unlikely hero in the form of an ex-convict hustling pirate DVDs.

Ma Jian's *Beijing Coma* (Chatto & Windus, 2008) tells the story of the post-Tiananmen generation through the experience of a man shot in the head during the protests, who is left musing about his life while China transforms around his comatose form. A similar approach, framing the last 30 years as collective amnesia about what really matters, can be found in Chan Koonchung's *The Fat Years* (Doubleday, 2011).

## The Land of Swallows

For the story of Pierre Teilhard de Chardin, his China expedition and his star-crossed love for Lucile Swan, see Amir Aczel's *The Jesuit and the Skull: Teilhard de Chardin, Evolution and the Search for Peking Man* (Riverhead Books, 2007). Gao Xing's *Peking Man Site at Zhoukoudian* (BPH, 2004) offers a good introduction to the archaeology of the site. Statistics in this chapter were taken from Gina Barnes's *The Rise of Civilization in East Asia: The Archaeology of China, Korea and Japan* (Thames & Hudson, 1999). My quotes in this chapter from the *Intrigues of the Warring States* are taken from J.I. Crump's *Chan-Kuo T'se* (University of Michigan, 1996).

## North and South

The translations from the *Ballad of Mulan* in this chapter are my own from the original Chinese, but you can read it in English in its entirety in Arthur Waley's *Chinese Poems* (new ed. Routledge, 2012). The story of the woman with several husbands is taken from *Women in Early Imperial China* (Rowman & Littlefield, 2002) by Brett Hinsch. For the story of Nezha, see E T C Werner's *Dictionary of Chinese Mythology* (Julian Press, 1961). Discussions of the architecture of the city and its uses in warding or encouraging spirits, rely upon Jeffrey Meyer's *The Dragons of Tiananmen: Beijing as a Sacred City* (University of South Carolina Press, 1991). For many customs and rituals from old Beijing, including the stories associated with the bridge of magpies, see Derk Bodde's *Annual Customs and Festivals in Peking as recorded in the Yen-ching Sui-shih-chi* (Henri Vetch, 1936). The story of 'Ruby' is from *Beijing Legends* by Jin Shoushen (Foreign Languages Press, 2005) – a compilation of folktales from throughout history, but favouring the Ming and Qing periods; it also forms an important source for my next three chapters.

## Khanbalikh

Timothy Brook's *The Troubled Empire: China in the Yuan and Ming Dynasties* (Harvard, 2010) offers a general introduction to the period, provocatively and entertainingly framed in terms of reports of 'dragons', which he cross-references with droughts and floods symptomatic of the 'Little Ice Age'. For an account of the Grand Canal that makes special reference to the labours of Guo Shoujing,

*China's Imperial Way* (Odyssey, 1997) by Kevin Bishop and Annabel Roberts traces the whole thing all the way from Hong Kong.

My quotes from Marco Polo's *Travels* use the out-of-copyright Henry Yule translation, but the reader with a genuine interest in a readable and critically edited version would do well to use Ronald Latham's (Penguin, 1958). For an assessment of Polo in historical context, Stephen Haw's *Marco Polo's China: A Venetian in the realm of Khubilai Khan* (Routledge, 2006) is an excellent study. My own books *Marco Polo* (Haus Publishing, 2007) and *A Brief History of Khubilai Khan* (Robinson, 2010) also offer histories of the 'Mongol' period in Beijing.


## The Forbidden City

For an in-depth treatment of the alleged relationship of Beijing to the transmogrified corpse of Nezha, the best source is Arlington and Lewisohn's *In Search of Old Peking* (see above). Qi Luo's bilingual *The Great Wall* (BPH, 2004) has some lovely pictures stories about the Ming dynasty's most enduring relic. Zhang Heshan's *Whispers from the Wall: Great Wall Folktales Told Across the Centuries* (China Intercontinental Press, 2009) is also in both Chinese and English, and as the title implies, is an unapologetically uncritical collection of any stories the author has heard about the subject.

For the Eight Great Sights, see Aldrich's *Vanishing Beijing* (HKUP, 2006). Hu Hansheng's *The Ming Tombs* (BPH, 2004) is a fine guide to the Ming necropolis, although its travel recommendations are understandably out of date – Hu cannot possibly have imagined that within little more than a decade, the site would be within reach of the Beijing subway.

For the Forbidden City, there are numerous books available – I have referred specifically to Leng Pu's *The Palace Museum* (BPH, 2004). As for the backstabbing and double-crossing of the emperor's harem, you can't do much better than Shang Xizhi's entertainingly tawdry *Tales of Empresses and Imperial Consorts in China* (Hai Feng, 1994).

For the complex and dramatic tale of Wu Sangui and his supposed treason, my own book *Coxinga and the Fall of the Ming Dynasty* (History Press, 2005) has it all in spades, as well as the prolonged aftermath, in which the last of the Ming loyalists held out for another 40 years.

Victor Meignan's *From Paris to Pekin Over Siberian Snows* (Swan Sonneschein and Co., 1885) is my source of quotes from the cantankerous French traveller. Paul Reinsch's *An American Diplomat in China* (Doubleday, Page and Co., 1922) is also quoted.

## 'Peking'

George Macartney's *An Embassy to China* (Longmans, 1962) has since been republished in a lavish Folio Society edition (2004).

Everybody and his dog wrote tell-all accounts of the larks they had in the Legation Quarter, particularly after the derring-do of the Boxer Rebellion. Diana Preston's *A Brief History of the Boxer Rebellion: China's War on Foreigners, 1900* (Robinson, 2002) is the standard modern work on the Rebellion itself and collates many primary sources. Readers who want to read actual correspondence can try the centenary edition of *The Siege of the Peking Embassy, 1900* (The Stationery Office, 2000). The future US president Herbert Hoover and his wife were also among the besieged legations – a story glossed in just a handful of pages in most biographies, but dealt with at greater length in Gary Nash's *The Life of Herbert Hoover: The Engineer 1874–1914* (Norton, 1983). Putnam Weale, a pseudonym for Bertram Lenox Simpson, published his own account of the siege and of the city in which it took place, as *Indiscreet Letters from Peking* (G. Bell, 1906). Notably, foreign accounts are usually big on the siege, and conspicuously more reticent about what Weale calls the 'sack' afterwards, when the Eight Powers Army looted the whole town.

The reader interested in the early 20th century is advised to start with Julia Boyd's *A Dance with the Dragon: The Vanished World of Peking's Foreign Colony* (I.B. Tauris, 2012), which offers glimpses of many primary sources, and will facilitate some considerable cherry-picking. Quotes in this book from Mrs Alec Tweedie, cattily entertaining and often presciently accurate, are from her book *An Adventurous Journey: Russia-Siberia-China* (Thornton Butterworth, 1926), which compared Beijing with the newly Bolshevik Moscow.

Some other quotes from this period are sourced from Ellen LaMotte's *Peking Dust* (Century, 1919), a book with great insights into the expat community of the time, and some apt commentary on the way the Chinese were being exploited by the European powers. LaMotte is particularly good on the opium trade, and on the forgotten 'Twelve Demands' issued by the British in 1917 with regard to Tibet.

Despite devoting much of its page-count to life in the Summer Palace rather than the place promised in its title, 'Princess' Der Ling's *Two Years in the Forbidden City* (Moffat, Yard and Co., 1911) is notable for its intimate and sympathetic portrait of the Empress Dowager as a capricious, deluded, but ultimately good-hearted old lady. It is loaded with some wonderful quotes from its subject, including 'Do you know, I have often thought that I am the most clever woman that ever lived,' and 'What is dancing?'

The most famous foreign resident of the period was arguably the man chronicled in Hugh Trevor-Roper's *Hermit of Peking: The Hidden Life of Sir Edmund Backhouse* (Penguin Books, 1978 – earlier editions lack useful revisions). Backhouse lives again, in all his scandalous glory, in *Décadence Mandchoue: The China Memoirs of Sir Edmund Trelawny Backhouse* (Earnshaw Books, 2011), Derek Sandhaus's painstakingly reconstructed edition of his sordid fantasies of life in the brothels of the old city. Australian readers may prefer Cyril Pearl's *Morrison of Peking* (Penguin Australia, 1970), which chronicles the life of the man who briefly lent his name to Wangfujing.

For a real insider's-eye view, of course, there's always 'Henry' Puyi's *From Emperor to Citizen: The Autobiography of Aisin-Gioro Pu Yi* (Foreign Languages Press, 1989), a Party-approved memoir by the famous Last Emperor, or at least by his ghost-writer Li Wenda (there are rumours that novelist Lao She also helped buff it up a bit). Reginald Johnston's *Twilight in the Forbidden City* (4th rev. ed., Soul Care, 2008) is less liable to have been redacted by a Party scrutineer.

## Northern Peace

Arlington and Lewisohn's *In Search of Old Peking* (1935, my references are to the 1967 edition from Paragon Book Reprint Corp.) deserves to be filed among the greatest of the general accounts above, but is listed here because it was written in the closing days of 'Northern Peace' and strongly reflects the city of that era. Written at roughly the same time, and imparting even greater detail for the reader of Chinese, is Ma Zhixiang's 1935 *Beiping Lüxing Zhinan* (*A Guide to Beiping for Travellers*) – the version I have referred to is the annotated modern edition, *Lao Beijing Lüxing Zhinan* (Yanshan, 1997).

Paul's French's *Midnight in Peking* (Viking, 2011) is an enthralling account of the last days of the old city, pertinently characterised by the gruesome murder of an unfortunate Russian refugee girl near the

Fox Tower. Meanwhile, as the subtitle suggests, John Blofeld's *City of Lingering Splendour: A Frank Account of Old Peking's Exotic Pleasures* (Hutchinson, 1961) is an uncensored account of his time as a young man in the city during the mid-1930s, crowded with drug addicts and fallen women, with the ominous clouds of war gathering in the northeast. For the origins of the May Fourth Movement, my own biography of the Chinese diplomat Wellington Koo (Haus, 2008) details his origins in late-Qing China, and the series of unfortunate events that led to his infamous refusal to sign the Treaty of Versailles in 1919.

## Empty Spaces

There are several lively accounts of life in the Communist era, including Patrick Wright's *Passport to Peking: A Very British Mission to Mao's China* (Oxford University Press, 2010). Delia Jenner's *Letters from Peking* (Oxford University Press, 1967) present an interesting snapshot of a young scholar's life in the Cultural Revolution period. Frances Wood's *Hand Grenade Practice in Beijing: My Part in the Cultural Revolution* (John Murray, 2000) is not quite the Spike Milligan romp promised by the title, but still engages amiably with the absurdities of its day. Perhaps the most unexpected chronicle of late Mao-era Beijing can be found in *The China Diary of George H.W. Bush* (Princeton, 2008), compiled by Jeffrey Engel from the notes and tapes of the man who was America's de facto China ambassador from 1974–5, before diplomatic relations officially thawed and the author went on to bigger things.

The best book on recent urban change is Michael Meyer's *The Last Days of Old Beijing: Life in the Vanishing Backstreets of a City Transformed* (Walker & Co., 2009), an account of hutong life by an American resident who provides copious details on the city's history, while also chronicling the advance of the bulldozers as the Olympics loomed.

## Beijing in the 21st Century

Anne-Marie Broudehoux's *The Making and Selling of Post-Mao Beijing* (Routledge, 2004) is particularly good on the politics of the Olympic bid and the changes wrought upon the city as a result.

At the risk of stating the obvious, modern life is happening all around you, and much of it has yet to be written up in volume form.

Rachel DeWoskin's *Foreign Babes in Beijing: Behind the Scenes of a New China* (Granta, 2005) is a snapshot of 21st-century life, by a PR consultant who inadvertently became a Chinese soap opera star. A more considered look at changes in modern Beijing, and perhaps changes to come, can be found in Stephanie Tansey's *Recovery of the Heart: Dialogues with People Working Towards a Sustainable Beijing* (New World Press, 2012). At times, it feels like the author has rounded up all her friends in a pub and called it research, but even so, there are many provocative and thought-provoking ideas here for a greener Beijing, and of the problems Beijing is liable to face in the interim.

Quirky and entertaining, *Hiking in Beijing* (Foreign Languages Press, 2010) is an update of a 2003 guide by a collective largely comprising foreign ramblers. Six years is a long time in the Beijing countryside, and some of its locations are liable to have been turned into yuppie enclaves by now, but it still offers an interesting account of country life in the shadow of the Great Wall.

## Eating and Drinking

There are surprisingly few books that genuinely grapple with the complex history and multiple kinds of 'Chinese' food. The best is *Food in China: A Cultural and Historical Enquiry* by Frederick J. Simoons (Telford Press, 1990); a wonderful history of the various changes in technology and ingredients, but an eye-stinging £102 and almost as expensive on the Kindle. E.N. Anderson's *The Food of China* (Yale University Press, 1990) is substantially cheaper, and liable to meet the needs of most.

Rather than get bogged down in weighing the merits of a bunch of contending cookbooks, I instead recommend Fuschia Dunlop's *Shark's Fin & Sichuan Pepper: a sweet-sour memoir of eating in China* (Ebury Press, 2008), a charming and occasionally gross account of one woman's love-affair with Chinese food.

Li Zhenping's *Chinese Wine: Universe in a Bottle* (China Intercontinental Press, 2009) is a lively narrative not only of the types of Chinese alcohol, but also of the customs and history associated with their consumption.